The Complete Mr. Moto
Film Phile: A Casebook

Peter Lorre as Mr. Moto

The Complete Mr. Moto Film Phile: A Casebook

Howard M. Berlin

WILDSIDE PRESS

The Complete Mr. Moto Film Phile: A Casebook

Published by:
Wildside Press, LLC
www.wildsidepress.com

"To recognize one's faults requires intelligence; to admit them requires courage."

—Mr. Moto

Contents

Preface

I guess I became a fan of the Mr. Moto films during the 1970s when local TV stations showed Charlie Chan films on their late-night "Charlie Chan Theater" shows and these sometimes included the Mr. Moto entries. I became strongly attracted to the Oriental detective films of Charlie Chan, Mr. Moto, and Mr. Wong, which seemed to have a lot going for them when compared with many of the other Hollywood detective films of the 1930s and 1940s.

As a outgrowth of my interest in the genre, I had previously written two books on Charlie Chan in the past year: *The Charlie Chan Films Encyclopedia* (McFarland, 2000) and *Charlie Chan's Words of Wisdom* (Wildside Press, 2001). The later contains about 600 of the pithy aphorisms attributed to the inscrutable Chinese detective. I then found out that most of the fans of *Charlie Chan* films also seemed to enjoy the *Mr. Moto* series, especially the ones with Peter Lorre. It then seemed a logical progression to write a *Mr. Moto* book. Although there were pieces of information about the *Mr. Moto* series here and there, there was no one single book that was entirely devoted to it. This book was written to fill that void—a reference bible for Mr. Moto film lovers everywhere.

The Complete Mr. Moto Film Phile: A Casebook is the culmination of my effort. It is divided into three major sections. The first is concerned with the three individuals that helped create and develop the *Mr. Moto* character: author John P. Marquand, actor Peter Lorre, and director/scenarist Norman Foster. This section gives the biographies of these three individuals, with emphasis on their contributions to the *Mr. Moto* novels and films. In addition, a character sketch of the *Mr. Moto* character is presented with comparisons between the character of Marquand's novels and that of Foster's films and a comparison between Charlie Chan and Mr. Moto.

The second part of the book is a film guide of the nine Mr. Moto films—the first eight stars Peter Lorre from 1937 to 1939, and the last entry, twenty-six years later in 1965, with Henry Silva. Each film provides information about cast and crew lists, running times, release dates, onscreen credits, notable facts, trivia, commentaries, posters, title cards, and stills. Because many of the films are not readily available on commercial video-tapes or DVD, the storylines are somewhat detailed to provide the reader, who might not have access to the films, with the many scene-by-scene details of the plots. My favorite film of the series is *Thank You, Mr. Moto* (1937) while my least favorite is *The Return of Mr. Moto* (1965).

The final section, sometimes referred to by publishers as the "back matter" of a book, includes an appendix which contains several useful items. Appendix A lists Marquand's published writings and also compares the titles of the *Mr. Moto* published serializations, books, and reissued paperbacks; Appendix B lists the alternate and working titles for all of the films in the Mr. Moto series; Appendix C lists those actors and actresses that appeared in two or more films; and Appendix D lists the wise sayings of Mr. Moto which are nowhere as numerous as those of Charlie Chan.

In researching the material for this book, I was quite surprised to learn that John P. Marquand, Mr. Moto's creator, and I have several things in common. First, we are both writers, although I will probably never be as famous as he was. Second, we both were born in Wilmington, Delaware. I pass the address where he lived, 1301 Pennsylvania Avenue, several times a week in the course of my travels. Both our fathers were engineers—his was a civil engineer, mine was a chemical engineer. Both of us majored in the sciences at college—Marquand studied chemistry, I studied electrical engineering with a minor in chemistry.

This book could not have been possible without the assistance of those who provided needed stills, photos, advice, and factual information. For those who were considerate and generous in sharing their time and resources, I would like to acknowledge the assistance of the following individuals:

Cary J. Black, Richard Bojarski, Claire Brandt (of Eddie Brandt's Saturday Matinee), Bill Christensen, Diane DiCarlo, Andy Gillihan, Ken Hanke, Lane R. Hirabayashi, Jim Kallgren, Cheryl Morris, Jeff Norman, Steve Rhodes, Larry Smith, Jim Spotts (of Rare Serials & B-Westerns), Jon Tuska, and Peter J. Vaskas.

As was with my two *Charlie Chan* books, I repeat my wish that I hopefully have done my homework better in writing this book than the villains did theirs in the films, for they were always caught or killed. Enjoy.

–Howard M. Berlin
Wilmington, Delaware

The Selling of Mr. Moto

The creation and development of the *Mr. Moto* character from its novels to the silver screen couldn't have been possible without the combined talents of three individuals. Novelist John P. Marquand gave life to the Japanese agent following a trip to the Orient where in Japan he was constantly shadowed by a polite little Japanese detective. Public interest and the death two years earlier of Charlie Chan's creator, Earl Derr Biggers, together would convince Marquand to make Mr. Moto an ongoing character.

The death of Biggers and the popularity of his *Charlie Chan* character caused Twentieth Century-Fox to adapt Marquand's character in what would be a popular series despite its short life. Producer Sol M. Wurtzel selected Norman Foster, then a neophyte junior director at the studio, for the responsibility to write the screenplay and direct the new enterprise. To

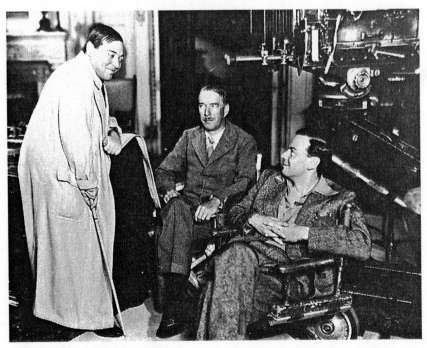

Lorre, Marquand, Foster

complete the needed elements, actor Peter Lorre, with his gnome-like stature, moon face, ping-pong eyes, and distinctive nasal voice, was chosen to play the title role. In hindsight of more than 60 years, it's hard to think of anyone who could play the role better than Lorre.

This section gives the biographies of these three individuals, with emphasis on their contributions to the *Mr. Moto* novels and films. In addition, a character sketch of the *Mr. Moto* character is presented with comparisons between the character of Marquand's novels and that of Foster's films, and a comparison between Charlie Chan and Mr. Moto.

John P. Marquand—Novelist

John P. Marquand— Novelist, 1893-1960

John Phillips Marquand often wrote gentle satires about the customs and habits of Boston's upper-class elite and was considered by many to have held an important place in American popular fiction from the early 1920s through the 1950s. Before he gained fame by winning a Pulitzer Prize, Marquand was a highly successful writer of adventure serials and short stories for magazines. Among these were the adventures of a Japanese character named Mr. Moto.

Although his ancestors had well-established roots in New England, some even with a pedigree, his father Philip, both a graduate of Harvard and a graduate civil engineer from M.I.T., took a job with the American Bridge Company in Wilmington, Delaware and it was there Philip's wife, Margaret Curzon Marquand, gave birth to their son on November 10, 1893. Considered somewhat of a snob by many, John P. Marquand later regretted being born in Delaware, feeling he was destined to be born in his beloved Boston instead.

Marquand once commented that "My father's greatest talent seemed to be a talent for losing money," a result of the 1907 stock market crash. As his father was constantly moving around the country looking for work, John was left to be raised with relatives in New England and much of his early life had been interrupted, hard and poor experiences which often shaped his later life and his writings. Once he had reached success, Marquand was often frugal despite his penchant for luxury. To some, Marquand's tighfistedness bordered on being an obsession.

When growing up, Marquand often resented having to attend public schools while many of his well-off distant relatives attended private boarding schools. For those from society's upper crust, there was no place other than Harvard to go to once they finished their secondary education. Marquand however wasn't so fortunate. His ordinary high school education didn't adequately prepare him for the Ivy League school's entrance exams like those who went to prep schools such as Exeter where students had the luxury of being coached for the exams. He failed parts of the exams three times and although graduating high school in 1910, he returned to high school classes for another year to improve his chances the next time he would take the exams.

If failing the entrance exams three times wasn't enough of a disappointment, the family had no money to send him to Harvard even if he finally did gain admission. He visited one of the area's prominent Harvard alumni to lobby for a Harvard Club Scholarship but got nowhere. Now running out of options, Marquand then applied for one of the Wheelwright Scholarships, a needs-based prize awarded to public school graduates who (1) should be Protestant and (2) must pursue a science curriculum in college. On his fourth try, Marquand passed the last of his entrance exams. He informed Harvard in June 1911 that he would major in chemistry and that his expenses would be paid by the Wheelwright Fund.

The social culture at Harvard meant belonging to the *right* clubs. If you didn't belong to one, you were a nobody. Despite his not being asked to join any club at Harvard, whose membership fees he couldn't afford anyway—being there on a scholarship, he nevertheless managed to make several friends and graduated in 1915. Following graduation, Marquand served in the army as a first lieutenant stationed on the U.S. border with Mexico and in France during World War I with an artillery brigade. The first-time experience of seeing the bloody nature of war left an everlasting impression on him, which would be the fodder for some of his successful war novels.

Following the 1918 Armistice and his discharge from the army, Marquand headed to New York for his first job as a feature writer for the *New York Herald*. At the suggestion of a friend, he later joined the J. Walter Thompson advertising agency as a copywriter for $60 a week, almost twice what he received at the *Herald*. One day in 1921 Marquand came across the *Saturday Evening Post*, a weekly magazine that contained lots of stories and a serialized novel in every issue. In his mind he felt that these kinds of stories were simple to write and essentially followed a formula story line. In one evening he typed out his first short story, *The Right That Failed*, with very little effort. He then submitted it to the *Saturday Evening Post*, who quickly bought it and published it in its July 23rd issue. Unknown to Marquand then, the *Post* would overwhelmingly be his primary outlet for his future writings.

In time however, the advertising agency's president bluntly told Marquand that he felt the copywriter did not have a knack for business and that he should look for a job elsewhere. Despite losing his job, he nevertheless felt relieved since he had already been able to publish several of his stories and could now pursue writing full-time. His formula story line that fitted the *Post's* style—that of a poor man who falls in love with a socially prominent and rich woman, or its converse—were eagerly gobbled up by the magazine's editors.

Marquand was then coaxed to write a full-length novel, *The Unspeakable Gentleman*, a 1922 romantic spy story which was first serialized in *Ladies' Home Journal* (February, March, May) and published by Charles Scribner's Sons in book form later that year. This would be the manner in which many of Marquand's books were marketed—a story first appears as a magazine serial and is then released as a trade book. Marquand's formula writing proved very successful. He was now a household name and many of the *Saturday Evening Post's* readers eagerly bought issues just to read his stories.[1] Carl Brandt, Marquand's literary agent, was now able to get his client from $500 to $3,000 for each of his *Post* stories and between $30,000 to $40,000 for each novel. Besides the *Post* and *Ladies' Home Journal*, Marquand was to write his fiction for many of America's "slick" mass-circulation magazines: *Collier's, Scribner's Magazine, Cosmopolitan, Woman's Home Companion, American Magazine, McCalls, Esquire, Life, Good Housekeeping, Harper's Bazaar, Harper's Magazine, Atlantic Monthly,* and *Sports Illustrated.*

Author Richard Wires in his book, *John P. Marquand and Mr. Moto: Spy Adventures and Detective Film,* notes the reason for Marquand's need to write:

---

1   In the early 1930s, the official circulation of the *Saturday Evening Post* stood at more than three million, with each issue costing five cents.

"There was also a compulsiveness in his approach to writing that arose from a fear of financial insecurity that persisted long after he had become wealthy. He could not resist the large sums of money readily earned by sale of undemanding stories to the mass-circulation magazines."

In 1934, Marquand's 12-year marriage to Christina Sedgewick, whose uncle was editor of the *Atlantic Monthly*, was failing and a divorce was granted on May 15, 1935. Earl Derr Biggers, the author who wrote five *Charlie Chan* novels which served as the basis for a popular series of movies for Twentieth Century-Fox, had died in April 1933. Seizing the opportunity to capitalize on the void left by Biggers' passing, *Saturday Evening Post* editor George Horace Lorimer asked Marquand to develop a replacement character to Biggers' inscrutable Oriental detective. To secure Marquand's commitment to the project, Lorimer plied his popular author both with expense money and a cash advance while sending him to visit the Orient to gather background material for his story. His deteriorating marital situation also helped swing the deal, and the trip would provide Marquand with a fresh outlook on things. Also about this time there were discussions between Marquand and Alfred M. McIntyre, his editor at Little, Brown and Company, about Marquand writing a "Boston" social satire, but this project would often be bogged down and delayed.

With the *Post's* sponsorship Marquand made two trips to the Orient. The first, in March 1934, was to Korea, Japan, Manchuria,[2] and China, with much of it in Peking. The first fruits of this journey was the short novel, *Ming Yellow*, a six-part serial that appeared in the *Saturday Evening Post* from December 8, 1934 to January 12, 1935. The story concerns an American caught up in the search of unseen valuable yellow porcelain, and is complicated by the presence of Chinese outlaws and warlords in northern China. The trade book, published by Little, Brown and Company, followed several months later.

---

2   The Chinese northern province of Manchuria was then known as Manchukuo, a Japanese puppet state after its 1931 conquest.

A second novel—Marquand's first to use the *Mr. Moto* character—was *No Hero*,[3] and it followed only a few months after *Ming Yellow* was published. The *Post* quickly serialized the story in six installments from March 30 through May 4, 1935 and Little, Brown and Company published it in book form shortly thereafter.[4]

As for how John P. Marquand came to create his obsequious Japanese character,[5] David Zinman in *Saturday Afternoon at the Bijou*, quotes Marquand:

> "I was sent to China in 1934 by the *Saturday Evening Post* with instructions to do a series of stories with an authentic Oriental background. Naturally, I did a great deal of poking around in Chinese cities and eventually wandered to Japan. There I was constantly shadowed by a polite little Japanese detective. Suddenly, it dawned on me that he was just the protagonist I was looking for—and while my shadow did his duty very conscientiously, 'Mr. Moto,' the shrewd, the polite, the efficient sleuth was born."

However, a slightly different explanation is given by Marquand in a 1957 *Newsweek* interview:

> "I wrote the Mr. Moto stories after a visit to the Orient more than twenty years ago. Curiously enough, Americans were much less popular in Japan in the early and mid-'30s than they appear to be today. I was constantly

---

3   It is interesting to note here that Richard Wires (*John P. Marquand and Mr. Moto: Spy Adventures and Detective Films*) points out that he is unable to explain why both two major Marquand biographers (Bell, p. 249; Birmingham, p. 305) make the same error, giving the serialization title as *Mr. Moto Takes a Hand* instead of *No Hero*.

4   Little, Brown and Company reprinted No Hero in 1985 as a paperback with the title, *Your Turn, Mr. Moto*. Apparently, the publisher's aim was to include the words "Mr. Moto" in order to unify the titles of the six original novels it published when they were reprinted as paperbacks in 1985 and 1986. Occasionally there is confusion among differences in the titles of the same novel. Appendix A summarizes the differences between the serialization, original book, and reprinted paperback titles.

5   A more detailed description of the Mr. Moto character is presented later in this book. See the section, "Mr. Moto—A Character Sketch."

followed by Japanese detectives who used to search my baggage very clumsily almost every night. They all looked and talked exactly like Mr. Moto."[6]

Marquand originally did not plan to make Mr. Moto a continuing character when he made his debut in *No Hero,* as was Charlie Chan. Many of the five sequels were written simply in response to huge reader interest. Carl Brandt was able to convince Twentieth Century-Fox to acquire the screen rights to *No Hero* in the Fall of 1935 but the studio never made a movie from the novel. Marquand had been only too glad to earn additional money by selling screen rights to his character and stories without being too concerned about how the film makers dealt with the *Mr. Moto* character. Author Joe Guilfoyle in the anthology, *Peter Lorre* (edited by Gary and Susan Svehla), recalls that in 1959, Marquand gave the following *mea culpa* about his well-known literary character:

> "Mr. Moto was my literary disgrace. I wrote about him to get shoes for my baby. I can't say why people still remember him."

As it would frequently be his style in the *Mr. Moto* sequels, *No Hero* is told in the third-person narrative. Kenneth C. Lee, called K.C. or Casey by his friends, narrates the story and through his eyes. Mr. Moto is first described as a short man with his hair cut after the "Prussian fashion." The reader is also told that Moto had been a valet in America and that he consumes whiskey like a man who had no faith in his alcoholic capacity so that he drinks in "small careful sips."

One item that often raises discussion among fans of both the *Mr. Moto* novels and films is the proper classification of what kind of fiction it is. Many have described the *Mr. Moto* series in the same breath as other popular contemporary detective stories of the '30s and '40s—Charlie Chan, Philo Vance, Boston Blackie, The Saint, the Crime Doctor, and Sherlock Holmes, to name several. However, the Mr. Moto of Marquand's novels

---

6   "Why Did Mr. Moto Disappear?" *Newsweek,* January 21, 1957, p. 106.

should not be considered a "detective" in the true sense, for he uses no talents that would warrant labeling him as such. Moto was an intelligence or counterespionage agent in the service of the Japanese emperor, and is somewhat similar to Ian Fleming's "Agent 007"—James Bond. Perhaps then, the *Mr. Moto* novels should be labeled as "spy stories," as the common setting throughout the series is that of international espionage. Marquand himself preferred to call his *Mr. Moto* novels "mysteries" while author Wires classifies the novels as "adventures." As for the movies, only two had any close connection to the novels. Of the remaining seven films (including the one with Henry Silva), only two could be accurately labeled as belonging to the detective genre: *Mr. Moto's Gamble* (1938) and *Mr. Moto in Danger Island* (1939).

China held a strong attraction for Marquand and a second trip there in 1935 following his divorce from Christina was made to update his background knowledge. But his travels also took Marquand away from working on his long-awaited social satire. Unlike his first trip to China, Marquand this time visited southern China, but soon returned to Peking in the north where the excitement was greater and the city provided him with new ideas for his second *Mr. Moto* story.

Marquand returned from his four-month sojourn to China in September. Although he promised McIntyre that he would resume work on his social satire, George Lorimer at the *Post* wanted a sequel to *No Hero*. As he realized early on in his career, the short adventure-type stories were easier to write and Marquand completed *Thank You, Mr. Moto* in about two months. The magazine reportedly paid him $30,000 for his effort and they immediately offered Marquand $40,000 for a third, forthcoming *Mr. Moto* manuscript. *Thank You, Mr. Moto* was serialized in the *Saturday Evening Post* from February 8 through March 14, 1936 (in six parts). Reluctantly, Alfred McIntyre again allowed *Thank You, Mr. Moto* to be published as a trade book following the serialization as an incentive to get Marquand back to writing *The Late George Apley*, a novel that was already taking more than two years to finish.

In *Thank You, Mr. Moto*, Tom Nelson, an American now living China who serves as the story's narrator, informs the reader about Moto's attitude towards bravery and loyalty: "A servant of the Emperor is not afraid of death. It is a glory to him when he serves his Emperor." Months later Marquand wrote his third *Mr. Moto* novel, *Think Fast, Mr. Moto*. It was serialized in the *Saturday Evening Post* from September 12 through October 17, 1936 (in six parts) and the trade book was published in 1937. In *Think Fast, Mr. Moto*, the reader is treated to the scope of Mr. Moto's abilities. Unabashedly he remarks:

> "I can do many, many things. I can mix drinks and wait on table, and I am a very good valet. I can navigate and manage small boats. I have studied at two foreign universities. I also know carpentry and surveying and know five Chinese dialects."

Like *No Hero*, Marquand also sold the film rights of his two 1936 *Mr. Moto* novels to Twentieth Century-Fox. This time however, Fox did go forward to make the first two films of its *Mr. Moto* series. For reasons that were never explained, films based on Marquand's second and third *Moto* novels were made in reverse order. Marquand was not a scenarist and the job of translating these two novels for the screen then fell upon both Howard Ellis Smith and Norman Foster, the latter who also directed these two films as well as four other films in the series.

In August 1937, Twentieth Century-Fox released *Think Fast, Mr. Moto* which featured the Hungarian-born actor Peter Lorre as Mr. Moto. Originally, this was to be the only *Mr. Moto* film, but to everyone's surprise, Peter Lorre and the film were well received by both the critics and movie goers. Producer Sol M. Wurtzel then ordered production of a second film, *Mr. Moto Takes a Chance* in July 1937 but the film was held up, probably because of the Sino-Japanese War.[7] Instead, production then began on *Thank You Mr. Moto* in October 1937 and the film was released in December 1937. Again Foster had reworked the novel, but this time with Willis Cooper. Except for their titles, the two films themselves bore little

---

7   *Mr. Moto Takes a Chance* was released in June 1938 as the fourth film in the series.

resemblance to Marquand's source novels. Even though he contributed little to the scripts of these two films, Marquand nonetheless reveled in his visits to Hollywood while the movies were in production. After these two novels, Hollywood would no longer rely on Marquand's novels as the source for future *Mr. Moto* films.

The year 1936 was to be one of Marquand's most productive, possibly fueled by his obsession with making money, rising from his fears of financial insecurity developed early on in his youth. Besides the two *Mr. Moto* novels, Marquand was busy turning out seven other non-*Moto* short stories for the *Post* that year. Also in the midst of writing his *Mr. Moto* novels, Marquand in 1936 finally found time to complete his long-awaited social satire. *The Late George Apley*—his "Boston novel" as he liked to call it—was started in 1934. When he finished it in the Fall of 1936, it was promptly serialized in the *Saturday Evening Post* from November 29, 1936 through January 9, 1937 (in seven installments); the trade book version was published just before the release of the *Think Fast, Mr. Moto* book. *The Late George Apley* would come to be one of the high points of Marquand's literary career, earning him the Pulitzer Prize in 1938.

Almost two years passed since the publication of *Think Fast, Mr. Moto* did Marquand start to begin writing his fourth *Mr. Moto* adventure. The invasion of northern China in 1937 by Japan may have had something to do with this such that a Japanese hero like Mr. Moto might not now have the appeal that it once did—even though the previous novels were popular and the two films enjoyed success. Nonetheless, *Mr. Moto Is So Sorry* was completed and quickly serialized in the *Saturday Evening Post* from July 2 through August 13, 1938 (in seven installments). One interesting piece of information in this book is the revelation of Moto's full name—I. A. Moto—although the meaning of the initials is never explained. It should be noted here though that Peter Lorre's cinematic character used the name "Kentaro Moto" as early as the first film, *Think Fast, Mr. Moto*. Only in Henry Silva's portrayal in *The Return of Mr. Moto* (1965) was the name I. A. Moto ever used in any of the nine *Mr. Moto* films. Once *Mr. Moto Is So Sorry* was released in book form, Little, Brown and Company then released the three-novel anthology, *Mr. Moto's Three Aces: A John P. Marquand Omnibus,* which contained the last three *Moto* novels: *Thank You, Mr. Moto*; *Think Fast, Mr. Moto*; and *Mr. Moto Is So Sorry*.

In 1941 much of Europe was involved in World War II and Japan's actions in Asia and the Pacific weren't much better. The loyal outlets that had previously and eagerly bought Marquand's submissions were now even more fearful of the wisdom of continuing to publish novels about a Japanese hero. Despite these concerns, Marquand finished his fifth *Mr. Moto* novel but the *Saturday Evening Post* wasn't interested. Instead, the manuscript was bought by *Collier's* with the condition that the "Mr. Moto" name not be part of the novel's title. The magazine then published the novel as *Macadam Island* from September 6 through October 25, 1941 (in eight installments) and Little, Brown and Company released it in 1942 in book form as *Last Laugh Mr. Moto*.

The five pre-war *Mr. Moto* novels provided one unexpected outgrowth of Marquand's Mr. Moto character. The name "Mr. Moto" was often used as a (perhaps pejorative) nickname for *all* Japanese by U.S. military personnel after Japan's attack on Pearl Harbor and was also used sporadically in commercial advertising. As one example, the Aeronca Aircraft Corporation of Middletown, Ohio published the following *Ode to Mr. Moto!* in the July 11, 1942 issue of *Collier's*, containing several terms that would probably be considered racist in today's climate:

> "Six Mitsubishis—with bombs all set to slide—
> The sailor gave his guns a squirt—and there were only five.
> Five Jap bombers thirsting still for gore,
> Our N.A. blipped another burst, and now—there's only four.
> Four grim and deadly Nipponese droned o'er the Eastern Sea,
> But one more crossed the 'ring sight'—then there were only three.
> Three gangsters still destruction bent, to wipe out ship and crew,
> Navy guns chattered a few times more—*Banzai!*—there's only two.
> And what's two Japs to a guy like that who's just grabbed his spot in the sun,
> So he poured on the coal with these Nips for his goal—
> Hell, shipmates—there's only one.
> One lone Jap on the Carrier intent, to crash decks aft—or fore,
> But our lad in the fighter wasted no time with this blighter,
> Now Moto doesn't live here any more."

Through the war years and beyond, Marquand continued to write novels satirizing Boston's upper-class society, just as he had successfully done in *The Late George Apley*. Some of his better known novels during this period were: *H. M. Pulham, Esquire* (1941) which was originally serialized as *Gone Tomorrow* by *McCall's* in 1940; *So Little Time* (1943); *B. F.'s Daughter* (1946); and *Point of No Return* (1949). In addition to the two *Mr. Moto* films, some of these novels were also made into films.[8]

It was now 1956 and it had been 15 years since Mr. Moto appeared in a magazine or book. Stuart Rose, the editor of the *Saturday Evening Post* contacted Marquand as to the possibility of writing another *Mr. Moto* novel. The war had been over for ten years and his readers probably would not have the same fears they had during World War II. Rose offered Marquand $5,000 for travel to the Far East in which to gather his material, plus an advance of $75,000. The circumstances of Marquand's marital life were almost the same too—his second wife, Adelaide Hooker Marquand, refused to give John a divorce and he looked at this trip as a temporary means of escape.

The trip lasted a month and Marquand completed his manuscript in the later part of 1956. He explained in his *Newsweek* interview the reason why his *Mr. Moto* disappeared for so long, first blaming it on the war but added:

> "I stopped because I wished to do something serious. I was tired of that literary form; it was all too easy. I revived Mr. Moto for my own amusement. It didn't take too long to write. I wanted to see whether or not I was still able to write a mystery, one of the most interesting forms of literary craftsmanship, if not art, that exists. I like to think that this is better than my early mystery stories; it ought to be, because I am twenty years older . . . I made up most of the secret-service business out of my own head; but then, it may be authentic. I assume no spy will ever write in."

---

8   *H. M. Pulham, Esquire* (1941, MGM), with Hedy Lamarr and Robert Young; *The Late George Apley* (1947, Twentieth Century-Fox), with Ronald Colman and Vanessa Brown; *B. F.'s Daughter* (1948, MGM), with Barbara Stanwyck and Van Heflin.

The finished manuscript was titled *Rendezvous in Tokyo* but the *Post* editors disliked the story's sad ending. Marquand stood firm and refused to make alterations to the ending, feeling now that the magazine editors were treating him, a Pulitzer Prize winner, shabbily. Realizing that they had already invested approximately $80,000 in the project, the *Post* editors eventually backed down and serialized the novel in eight parts from November 24, 1956 through January 12, 1957. Little, Brown and Company, as it was their custom with Marquand's previous books, published the book in 1957 after its serialization, but under the title of *Stopover: Tokyo*. When the publisher reprinted the novel in paperback form in 1986, the title was again changed, this time to *Right You Are, Mr. Moto*, in keeping with the trend of including the words "Mr. Moto" as a means of unifying the titles of the six original novels it published when they were reprinted as paperbacks. Also in 1957, Twentieth Century-Fox produced the film, *Stopover Tokyo*, featuring Robert Wagner and Joan Collins. Unlike Marquand's novel, the movie title had no colon and there was no character named Mr. Moto.

In the remaining years of his life, John P. Marquand combined his production of short stories with rekindling some of the ties he established or was prevented from establishing in his early years. Because he was now a noted author of American fiction, doors that were once closed to him were now open. Marquand was a member of Harvard Board of Overseers, a judge for the Book-of-the-Month Club, listed in Boston's *Social Register*, and belonged to some of the Boston social clubs he satirized.

Following dinner with his son John, Jr. one evening, Marquand went to bed and died during the night on July 16, 1960 at the age of 66,

Peter Lorre, 1904–1964

Peter Lorre—Actor

The Carpathian Mountains have produced their share of tales of horror as well as those actors that were suitable for these roles. Probably the most notable example was Hungarian-born Béla Lugosi who will forever be associated with the Dracula legend in the namesake role that made him famous. Right behind Lugosi would have to be Peter Lorre, with his gnome-like stature, moon face, ping-pong eyes, and distinctive nasal voice. With the possible exception of Edward G. Robinson, no actor has so often been the target of impressionists as is Peter Lorre. It is amazing that, despite having appeared in over 80 films and appearing with well-known horror-genre actors such as Boris Karloff, Béla Lugosi, Lon Chaney, Jr., and Vincent Price, Peter Lorre by his own definition of "horror" claimed to have made only a *single* horror picture—*The Beast with Five Fingers* (1946).

Lorre was born Ladislav (a.k.a. László) Löwenstein on June 26, 1904 in Rózsahegy, Hungary, then part of the Austro-Hungarian Empire,[9] and was the oldest child of Alois and Elvira Löwenstein. It is said that Lorre's expressive eyes, which would eventually come to project virtually every conceivable kind of emotion in his films, were inherited from his mother. When Peter was four years old, his mother died of blood poisoning only a few weeks after giving birth to their third son. Soon thereafter, Alois married Elvira's best friend, Melanie Klein to provide a mother for all the children.

As a teenager, Peter preferred painting and acting to schoolwork. Although Alois wanted Peter to pursue a profession that would provide a steady income, the two nonetheless reached a compromise whereby Peter promised that he would enter a business school, then get a job, and not quit. In exchange, his father allowed Peter to act in his spare time.

---

9   The Hungarian town of Rózsahegy, also called Rosenberg during the Austro-Hungarian Empire, is now in the Slovak Republic and is called Rízomberok.

Lorre in his cinematic debut in *M* (1931) as the child murderer Hans Beckert.

The theater was a magnetic attraction for Lorre. He was often admitted to theaters for free by agreeing to act as a shill—serving as an "applauder" to guarantee standing ovations. In time, Lorre met Jacob Moreno, who had founded what was called an "impromptu theater" and who had given Lorre a chance to develop his fledgling career. By the time he was about 20, Lorre developed a spontaneous, or improvisational style of acting. It was then that Moreno gave young Ladislav Löwenstein the stage name of Peter Lorre.

Over the next four years, Lorre appeared in theater productions in Vienna, Breslau, Zurich, and finally Berlin. While in the German capitol, a friend urged Lorre to approach playwright Bertolt Brecht to audition for the role of Fabian, the village idiot, in the upcoming play, *Pioniere in Ingolstadt* ("Engineers in Ingolstadt"). To Brecht, Lorre was the ideal person to make the required facial and body gestures and when the play opened in April 1929, Lorre was an instant success.

Lorre had chronic medical problems in his early years on the stage, especially with his gall bladder. Morphine was liberally used to help control the pain and allowed him to continue acting. However, a subsequent attack of appendicitis required removal of his gall bladder and required even more morphine for pain control. Lorre soon became addicted to the morphine, which also affected his overall health, and caused him to stop working for periods of time. Eventually, his teeth became rotten and he had them removed, being replaced by dentures.

For the next two years Lorre appeared in various German-language theater productions, such as *Frühlings Erwachen*—"Spring's Awakening," which were philosophic psychodramas concerned with murder, terror, satire, or sexual themes. Often in leading roles, Lorre's success on the stage had caught everyone's attention including the director Fritz Lang, who attended a rehearsal of *Frühlings Erwachen* and talked to Lorre.

Lang was convinced that Lorre was the right actor to star in his first talkie, *M* (a.k.a. *Mörder Unter Uns*—"Killer Among Us," 1931), in which Lorre was to portray Hans Beckert, a psychopathic child killer. When the film was released, the public reaction was enthusiastic and Lorre was an overnight success. As he would often be associated with terror and roles of tormented individuals throughout the rest of his career, Lorre's realistic portrayal had convinced many viewers that Lorre was a real Hans Beckert, prompting occasional calls to the police when Lorre was seen in public. Also, it was Lorre's image from *M* that was unwittingly used on the German poster for Fritz Hippler's 1940 Nazi anti-Semitic propaganda film, *Der Ewige Jude* ("The Eternal Jew").

Following his highly acclaimed success in *M*, Lorre for the next two years performed in a string of German-language films, mostly for Germany's *Universum-Film Aktiengesellschaft* (UFA). However, during this same period in Germany, Hitler's Nazi party was gaining strength through the ballot box and Hitler was finally made Chancellor of Germany in January 1933. Shortly thereafter, personal freedoms were virtually eliminated and the systematic persecution of liberals, academics, actors, and ethnic minorities—both German and non-German such as Jews and Gypsies—had begun.

In the weeks following the Reichstag fire of February 27, 1933, Hitler now had complete control as dictator. Seeing the writing on the wall with the purging of non-Germans, especially Jews, from making films, Lorre immediately left for Vienna with producer Sam Spiegel and actor Oskar Homolka. Once there, Lorre appeared in Spiegel's film, *Unsichtbare Gegner* ("Invisible Opponent"), in the minor role of a henchman.

In early 1934, Alfred Hitchcock was back in England at Gaumont-British Studios and was looking for an actor to play the role of Abbot, the terrorist in his suspense film, *The Man Who Knew Too Much* (1934). The studio, having learned that Lorre was out of work in Paris, suggested to Hitchcock that he consider Lorre for the role. Lorre came to England to meet with Hitchcock, who was not aware that Lorre spoke or understood no English, except for *yes* and *no*. When they met, Hitchcock spoke to Lorre first in the German he had learned when he had earlier worked for UFA, but soon conducted the rest of the one-sided conversation in English. Lorre couldn't understand Hitchcock's English at all but he could read the master director's facial expressions and mannerisms, correctly guessing when to nod, say *yes*, or laugh at the punch line of a story or joke. This guessing game apparently worked as Hitchcock hired Lorre for his first English-language picture. Lorre, who spoke only Hungarian and German, had to learn his English-language lines phonetically and then memorize them for the film. To his benefit and credit, Lorre quickly learned English. Lorre was concerned that he would be typecast and longed both for the chance to play a good guy and to be able to demonstrate his full range of talent.

Later in 1934, Lorre came to the United States and was now under contract to Harry Cohn at Columbia Pictures. Despite his being paid a weekly salary, no roles were forthcoming. Columbia then loaned Peter to MGM for his American acting debut where he portrayed the love-obsessed surgeon Dr. Gogol in *Mad Love* (1935), a remake of the 1925 German silent film, *Orlacs Hände* ("The Hands of Orlac"). Later that year, Lorre played the killer Roderick Raskolnikov in *Crime and Punishment* (1935), and was loaned to Hitchcock in England for a role as the assassin known as "The Hairless Mexican" in *Secret Agent* (1935). Despite Cohn's earlier promises, Columbia now felt that Lorre's talents were those that would constantly present casting problems and would be better suited to horror films, as was the case with Béla Lugosi. Because of these differences, Lorre left Columbia in 1936.

Fortunately for Lorre, he was quickly picked up by Twentieth Century-Fox, a new studio just recently formed in 1935 by the merger of William Fox's Fox Film Company and Joseph Schenck's Twentieth Century Pictures. Naturally he was gun-shy from his recent experience at Columbia, but Lorre was assured by Darryl Zanuck that the studio would find roles more to Lorre's liking. In *Crack-Up* (1936), Lorre finally got a chance to display the range of his talent, from the comedic to the sinister, when he played a merciless master spy named Randolph Maximilian Taggart who goes around disguised as "Colonel Gimpy," a feeble-minded, bugle-blowing mascot of a large airport.

In the 1930s, Twentieth Century-Fox had a successful *Charlie Chan* series staring Warner Oland as the inscrutable Oriental detective. Hoping for a similar success at the box office, the studio bought the film rights to a 1935 novel about another Oriental sleuth—this time a Japanese—written by John P. Marquand and serialized in the *Saturday Evening Post*. Like the Charlie Chan series, the studio continued the Hollywood practice of casting non-Orientals in leading roles—imagine, a Hungarian playing a Japanese! However, Lorre's small stature, bulging eyes, some makeup, and steel-rimmed glasses would transform the actor into a physical character not much different than the Mr. Moto of Marquand's novels.

Prior to the filming the first *Mr. Moto* entry, producer and writer Norman Foster had first met Peter Lorre at, of all places, a sanitarium to go over the future film. Lorre was institutionalized as a result of his addiction to morphine from an earlier bout with appendicitis and removal of his gall bladder. Compared to Charlie Chan, the Mr. Moto role was more physically demanding but Lorre never performed any of the stunts in his eight films. Instead, the stunts were performed at various times by Harvey Perry and John Kascier.

Director Vincent Sherman in his book, *Studio Affairs: My Life as a Film Director*, always had anecdotes about the goings on during the making of his films and other events, and Peter Lorre was no exception. In one situation, Sherman questions Lorre, "How did you do all those Mr. Motos at Fox?" Lorre responded, "I took dope!" At first, the people in attendance thought Lorre was joking but Sherman relates another incident that occurred several months later while attending a dinner party at Rudi Fehr's house. After Sherman tells the story for laughs, Fehr then shocks everyone by confirming Lorre's use of narcotics—"But he *did* . . . He took dope all during the making of the series." Suddenly, no one was laughing anymore.

In August 1937, Twentieth Century-Fox released *Think Fast, Mr. Moto.* Originally, this was to be the only *Mr. Moto* film, but to everyone's surprise, Peter Lorre and the film were well received by both the critics and movie goers. Many of the studio's stable of actors, contract players, and crew members who had worked on the *Charlie Chan* series were involved in the *Mr. Moto* undertaking as well. Based on the success of the initial entry, Sol Wurtzel two months later decided to go with filming a second film, *Thank You, Mr. Moto,* which was based on Marquand's second novel of the same name. With the exception of *Lancer Spy* (1937) and *I'll Give a Million* (1938), which were the studio's weak attempts to provide Lorre with meaningful roles, Lorre's next two years were exclusively relegated to making six additional films for the now popular series: *Mr. Moto's Gamble* (1938); *Mr. Moto Takes a Chance* (1938); *Mysterious Mr. Moto* (1938); *Mr. Moto's Last Warning* (1939); *Mr. Moto in Danger Island* (1939); and *Mr. Moto Takes a Vacation* (1939). However, Lorre again was concerned that he was risking being typecast and would never have the opportunity to appear in roles that befitted his talents. At least for now he was playing a good guy, albeit, a good guy who sometimes killed his enemies without remorse when he had to.

This frantic pace had quite an effect on Lorre's health—both physical and mental. He would often remain in his dressing room to get some rest and read between shootings. He also often listened to radio speeches by Adolph Hitler which sent him into bouts of depression. In a well-known anecdote during the filming of one *Mr. Moto* picture, Norman Foster came to Lorre's dressing room to remind him about an upcoming scene. Lorre then blurted out in anguish, "The whole world is falling apart, and you want me to make a picture!" As Lorre had escaped Germany because he was an actor, Jewish, and had a satirical sense of humor, it was hard to understand how he could portray a Nazi officer in *Lancer Spy*, although he did appear later in several anti-Nazi films.

In July 1939 following the release of the eighth *Mr. Moto* film, Lorre obtained a release from his contract with Twentieth Century-Fox, even though the studio had him under contract through 1940. There had been several proposed theories as to why the series ended when it did. One was the rise of anti-Japanese feelings following Japan's military expansion in Asia—the takeover of Manchuria and their "Rape of Nanking" in China. Another was that Norman Foster, who both directed and had a hand in writing six of the eight entries, wanted to move up to directing A-pictures. It was perhaps Lorre himself who finally pulled the plug, having felt betrayed by Twentieth Century-Fox's original promise to cast him in suitable roles.

Peter Lorre had now twice left studios after their failure to properly use his range of acting talent despite their assurances to the contrary. Although he would not know it then, the *Mr. Moto* experience would be a relative high point of his film career as he would unfortunately continue to receive typecast roles as a freelance actor in such unmemorable movies as: *Strange Cargo* (1940); *I Was an Adventuress* (1940); *Island of Doomed Men* (1940); *Stranger on the Third Floor* (1940); *You'll Find Out* [a.k.a. *Here Come the Boogie Men*] (1940); and *The Face Behind the Mask* (1941).

In 1941, neophyte director John Huston, who had been impressed by Lorre's performance in *M* ten years earlier, gave Lorre a chance to showcase his talent. Despite some misgivings by the Warner Bros. brass, Huston cast Lorre as the gardenia-scented, effeminate thief Joel Cairo in the remake of *The Maltese Falcon*, where he played alongside Humphrey Bogart, Mary Astor, and Sydney Greenstreet.[10] Although the movie was successful with three Oscar nominations, Lorre still did not receive fulfilling roles in

---

10   The original *The Maltese Falcon* (a.k.a. *Dangerous Female*), was made by Warner Bros. in 1931 and featured Ricardo Cortez as Sam Spade (later portrayed by Humphrey Bogart).

Even though Peter Lorre claimed he made only one horror picture in his career, he was always associated with the genre. Here he teams up with well-known horror meisters Béla Lugosi and Boris Karloff in a publicity pose for *You'll Find Out* (1940).

future projects.

It is not clear if Lorre was signed to a Warner Bros. contract prior to the filming of *The Maltese Falcon* even though Lorre at some time later did have a contract from the studio. Author Stephen Youngkin in his book, *The Films of Peter Lorre* writes, "Although Lorre drew Warner Bros.' attention in *The Maltese Falcon*, it did not earn him any commitment from the studio. Warners remained skeptical. In time, Lorre would become a fixture at the studio. He would even find a home and a family there. But the security that he enjoyed came only one film at a time." On June 2, 1943, Warner Bros. signed Lorre to a one year contract with renewable options. Contrary information is found in the anthology, *Peter Lorre*, edited by Gary and Susan Svehla. Gary Svehla writes, ". . . it was the first film on Peter Lorre's Warner Bros. contract (which would be terminated in 1946 after completing *The*

Verdict)."

Whether he had a studio contract or not, in 1942 Lorre again found himself with Bogart and Greenstreet in the classic *Casablanca*, a film that won three Oscars and five nominations. As Ugarte, an opportunist who forges exit visas for Nazi refugees, Lorre's involvement would be just two scenes and required only four days on the set. On the heels of the success of *Casablanca* at the box-office and the Academy Awards, Warner Bros. two years later churned out two similar anti-Nazi films with Lorre: *Passage to Marseille* (1944) and *The Conspirators* (1944). Despite appearing in no less than four films each year at Warners, the genre films—detective, horror, and war, which had been a staple of American cinema—had apparently run its course and the studio now found it increasingly more difficult to cast Lorre in roles befitting his talents.

Longing for work, Lorre in frustration declared that he would play virtually anything, and Jack Warner, whom Peter disliked, saw the chance to call Lorre's bluff. Lorre was given the role of Hilary Cummins, a psychopath, in *The Beast with Five Fingers* (1946)—Lorre's only horror picture, according to his own definition of the genre. After making 15 films with Warner Bros., Lorre's contract option was not renewed.

Following his release from Warner Bros., Lorre was encouraged to form Lorre Incorporated, thereby giving himself the power to control future roles and perhaps the opportunity to make his own film someday. Despite the optimism this new venture brought, no studios were beating a path to his door. To generate income in the meanwhile, Lorre toured the country performing selections from the horror stories of Edgar Allen Poe.

Even though Lorre was often concerned about being typecast, during the 1930s and 1940s he did gain some measure of success in another media—radio. Like several other villains of the silver screen, Lorre had a distinctive voice that was ideal for radio. In 1936, he debuted on *The Fleischmann Hour* as the diabolical Dr. Millaire. Other shows followed such as: *Suspense, Creeps by Night, Inner Sanctum, Mystery Playhouse,* and *Mystery in the Air*. The latter show was perhaps Lorre's greatest, allowing him to showcase his dramatic talent. In the early 1950s the growth of television sounded the death knell for many radio programs, and Peter Lorre's performances were no exception, save for a short stint hosting and narrating Mutual's *Nightmare* in 1953.

While in Germany, an old friend told Lorre about the story of a doctor who committed suicide and his assistant had been found dead—both men had lived at a refugee camp under false identities. Lorre's friend, a journalist, finally uncovered the background about the doctor, a Nazi scientist named Dr. Karl Rothe, whose unexplained remorse had caused him to murder his assistant and take his own life. This story then gave Lorre the impetus for his long awaited film—*Der Verlorene* ("The Lost One"), which Lorre served as director, writer, producer, and actor.

In September 1951, *Der Verlorene* played to small audiences. Because Germany was in the midst of reconstruction following its crushing defeat in World War II, a film of this type was not something the German people accepted with any measure of enthusiasm. In fact, most Germans found it depressing and morbid. The rejection of his film, the one he waited so long to do, had been a devastating blow to Lorre and he returned to the United States in 1952.

Now about 100 pounds heavier than when he starred in the *Mr. Moto* series, Lorre was now cast in character roles that tended to demean both his character and skills although there were a few exceptions: the role as Conseil in Walt Disney's version of *20,000 Leagues Under the Sea* (1954) and as Skeeter the clown in *The Big Circus* (1959). His forgettable performances would include: *Meet Me in Las Vegas* (1956); *Around the World in 80 Days* (1956); *The Story of Mankind* (1957); *The Sad Sack* (1957); *Voyage to the Bottom of the Sea* (1961); and *Five Weeks in a Balloon* (1962).

In 1962, Lorre was offered a role in "The Black Cat" segment of a three-part horror-spoof comedy, *Tales Of Terror* (a.k.a. *Poe's Tales of Terror*), which also featured Vincent Price. The following year had Lorre in two more spoofs: *The Raven* (1963) with Price and Boris Karloff, and *The Comedy of Terrors* (1963) with Price, Karloff, and Basil Rathbone. Lorre's last months however brought little satisfaction where he made what amounted to token guest appearances in his final two films: *Muscle Beach*

Lorre shows his rare comedic side as he clowns around with Vincent Price and Boris Karloff for a publicity shot on the set of The Raven (1963).

Party (1964) and *The Patsy* (1964).

On March 23, 1964, Peter Lorre died of a cerebral hemorrhage.[11] He had been separated from his third wife, Annemarie Brenning, since October 1962, and ironically, a divorce hearing had been scheduled for the same day he died.

---

11   Another source attributes Lorre's death to a heart attack.

Clockwise from the upper left: Peter Lorre as Dr. Gogol in *Mad Love* (1935); the Stranger in *Stranger on the Third Floor* (1940); Joel Cairo in *The Maltese Falcon* (1941); and Major Sigfried Gruning in *Lancer Spy* (1937).

Peter Lorre
Filmography

M (1931)

Bomben auf Monte Carlo (1931)

Die Koffer des Herrn O. F. (1931)

Fünf von der Jazzband (1932)

Schuß im Morgengrauen (1932)

F.P. 1 Antwortet Nicht (1932)

Der Weiße Dämon (1932)

Stupéfiants (1932)

Was Frauen Träumen (1933)

Unsichtbare Gegner (1933)

Du Haut en Bas (1933)

The Man Who Knew Too Much (1934)

Mad Love (1935)

Crime and Punishment (1935)

Secret Agent (1935)

Crack-Up (1937)

Nancy Steele Is Missing (1937)

Think Fast, Mr. Moto (1937)

Lancer Spy (1937)

Thank You, Mr. Moto (1937)

Mr. Moto's Gamble (1938)

Mr. Moto Takes a Chance (1938)

I'll Give a Million (1938)

Mysterious Mr. Moto (1938)

Mr. Moto's Last Warning (1939)

Mr. Moto in Danger Island (1939)

Mr. Moto Takes a Vacation (1939)

Strange Cargo (1940)

I Was an Adventuress (1940)

Island of Doomed Men (1940)

Stranger on the Third Floor (1940)

You'll Find Out (1940)

The Face Behind the Mask (1941)
Mr. District Attorney (1941)
They Met in Bombay (1941)
The Maltese Falcon (1941)
All Through the Night (1942)
Invisible Agent (1942)
The Boogie Man Will Get You (1942)
Casablanca (1943)
Background to Danger (1943)
The Constant Nymph (1943)
The Cross of Lorraine (1943)
Passage to Marseille (1944)
The Mask of Dimitrios (1944)
Arsenic and Old Lace (1944)
The Conspirators (1944)
Hollywood Canteen (1944)
Hotel Berlin (1945)
Confidential Agent (1945)
Three Strangers (1946)
Black Angel (1946)
The Chase (1946)
The Verdict (1946)
The Beast with Five Fingers (1946)
My Favorite Brunette (1947)
Casbah (1948)
Rope of Sand (1949)
Quicksand (1950)
Double Confession (1950)
Der Verlorene (1951)
Beat the Devil (1954)
20,000 Leagues Under the Sea (1954)
Meet Me in Las Vegas (1956)
Congo Crossing (1956)
Around the World in 80 Days (1956)
The Buster Keaton Story (1957)
Silk Stockings (1957)
The Story of Mankind (1957)
Hell Ship Mutiny (1957)

The Sad Sack (1957)
The Big Circus (1959)
Scent of Mystery (1960)
Voyage to the Bottom of the Sea (1961)
Tales of Terror - "The Black Cat" segment (1962)
Five Weeks in a Balloon (1962)
The Raven (1963)
The Comedy of Terrors (1964)
Muscle Beach Party (1964)
The Patsy (1964)

Norman Foster, 1900–1976

Norman Foster—
Director and Scenarist

The third major player in the development of the *Mr. Moto* film series is writer and director Norman Foster, who was born Norman Hoeffer on December 13, 1900 in Richmond, Indiana. Not much is known about Foster's early life except that he was a journalist and had turned to stage acting. In 1926 he appeared in productions such as *The Barker*, *Night Hostess*, and *June Moon*. In 1928 he married actress Claudette Colbert and one year later, was noticed in a Broadway play which earned him a contract with Paramount for a leading role in his first film directed by Millard Webb, *Gentlemen of the Press* (1929). In 1930, he and wife Claudette appeared in their only film together, *Young Man of Manhattan* (1930), a film probably remembered more for the screen debut of Ginger Rogers.

As an actor of almost 50 films, he appeared in both leading and supporting roles in B-pictures as the shy type rather than the dominant leading man. In the early 1930s, Foster's more memorable roles were in films such as *State Fair* (1933) with Will Rogers, John Ford's *Pilgrimage* (1933), and *Professional Sweetheart* (1934), again with Ginger Rogers. Strangely, Foster and Claudette never lived together and were divorced in 1935.[12]

In 1936, Foster got his chance at directing with *I Cover Chinatown* (1936), an independent film shot in San Francisco in which he also had an acting role. The following year, Foster married actress Sally Blane (born Elizabeth Jane Young) who was the older sister of film star Loretta Young.

In March 1935, the *Saturday Evening Post* began its serialization of the first of John P. Marquand's novels about the adventures of a Japanese agent, I. A. Moto. Twentieth Century-Fox was currently producing a suc-

---

12   Many cinematic sources cite the divorce in 1935, but Jean-Pierre Coursodon, in *American Directors*, gives the divorce as 1933.

cessful *Charlie Chan* series and saw the possibility of a similar appeal for Mr. Moto. The studio then bought the film rights to the *Mr. Moto* character from Marquand with the intent of making a single picture, and if the public liked it, then develop it into a series.

Author Jon Tuska in his book, *The Detective in Hollywood*, recounts a telephone interview he had with Sally, as Norman had laryngitis. Foster was nearby and Sally relayed his answers to Tuska's questions. At this time, Sally was pregnant and both she and Norman were planning a move to New York to look for work on the stage.

"Sol [Wurtzel] really did us a favor," Sally said. "He asked Norm, 'How does Sally feel about going to New York with a baby?' 'She doesn't like it,' Norm told him. Sol suggested that Norm become a director at Fox and Norm took him up on it. He started for $350 a week, when he had been getting $2,000 a week as an actor."

For this project, Producer Sol M. Wurtzel originally chose Kenneth McGowan to be in charge but he declined. Then Wurtzel picked Foster, a "junior" director who just finished directing *Fair Warning* (1937) for Wurtzel's B-movie factory as the helmsman to direct and convert Marquand's third novel, *Think Fast, Mr. Moto*, into a suitable screenplay. However, Foster wanted no part of Mr. Moto or any other low-budget assignment but reality told him that he had to start somewhere and make his mark if the choice projects were to be forthcoming.

At first, Foster was leery of Peter Lorre's selection, then a Fox contract player, for the role of Mr. Moto. After all, how could a Hungarian pass for a Japanese? Foster had first met Lorre prior to the filming the first Mr. Moto entry at a sanitarium to go over the future film. Lorre was institutionalized as a result of his addiction to morphine from an earlier bout with appendicitis and removal of his gall bladder. Following that meeting, Foster then recognized that Lorre's short stature closely paralleled the *Mr. Moto* of Marquand's novels and that perhaps with some makeup, glasses, and false buck teeth, Lorre could be a convincing character.

Besides his initial concerns about Lorre, Foster felt that Marquand's novel needed extensive overhauling for its transition to the screen. He then co-wrote the screenplay with Howard Ellis Smith and except for the film's title, much of the film bore little resemblance to the source novel. Nevertheless, the film was well received by the critics and the public. Wurtzel then ordered a second film, this time based on Marquand's second novel, *Thank You Mr. Moto*. Again Foster reworked the novel, but this time with Willis Cooper. Many critics feel that this film is the best of series.

In all, Norman Foster directed six of the eight *Mr. Moto* films. The two *Mr. Moto* films he did not direct were *Mr. Moto's Gamble* (1938), a reworked version of *Charlie Chan at the Ringside* that was never completed when Warner Oland died, and *Mr. Moto in Danger Island* (1939). For these two, Foster's absence was quite evident. Beside the first two films, Foster also co-wrote the screenplay for three additional films, all with Philip MacDonald: *Mysterious Mr. Moto* (1938); *Mr. Moto's Last Warning* (1939); *Mr. Moto Takes a Vacation* (1939); and wrote the original story for *Mr. Moto Takes a Chance* (1938) with Willis Cooper, a film considered near the bottom of the series.

During the same time Wurtzel was producing the *Mr. Moto* series at Twentieth Century-Fox, he also was producing the popular *Charlie Chan* series. Wurtzel also had Foster direct three *Charlie Chan* films with Sidney

Carol Lombard with Norman Foster in *Up Pops the Devil* (1931).

Toler: *Charlie Chan in Reno* (1939); *Charlie Chan at Treasure Island* (1939); and *Charlie Chan in Panama* (1940)—the last two, many fans consider the best of the *Chan* series. Incidentally, Foster had his wife Sally play the role of Stella Essex in *Charlie Chan at Treasure Island* which featured Cesar Romero (as the murderer). Clearly, Foster had now proven himself to be more than a "competent" B-film director.

Unlike the *Mr. Moto* series, where he was instrumental in the development of the series as a writer or scenarist and its director, Norman Foster had far less control in his three Chan films than he was given in the *Mr. Moto* series. The *Charlie Chan* series, first with Warner Oland and then with Sidney Toler following Oland's death in 1938, was already a well-established, popular series with 17 films when Foster was asked to direct *Charlie Chan in Reno*. Despite this established pattern, Ken Hanke in his book, *Charlie Chan at the Movies*, noted that this did not prevent Foster "from infusing much of himself into the proceedings and, as a result, his three Chan films boast his typical speed and self-deflating sense of invoke humor, making them very agreeable indeed."

In the early 1940s, Norman Foster became good friends with Orson Wells, a "boy wonder" in Hollywood. Wells was planning a four-episode "North American" saga, *It's All True*, with RKO. He had seen some of Norman's work and was impressed by them. In 1941 he wanted Foster to go to Mexico to direct one of the episodes—*My Friend Benito*. Unfortunately, this project was soon scrubbed and Wells had Foster return to the States to finish directing *Journey Into Fear* (1942), a film project Wells had intended to both produce and direct, but just didn't have the time to keep the production on schedule and budget.

After *Journey Into Fear* was completed, Foster returned to Mexico with offers to direct Spanish-language films. There he both wrote and or directed seven films that were well-received by the local press: *Santa* (1943), *La Fuga* (1943), and *La Hora de la Verdad* (1945), all three in which his brother-in-law, Ricardo Montalban appeared;[13] *La Casa Embrujada* (1944);

---

13   Ricardo Montalban in 1944 married Georgiana Young, the older sister of

El Ahijado de la Muerte (1946); and *El Canto de la Sirena* (1948).

Following his second return from Mexico, Foster often found himself again writing the screenplay *and* directing, this time for such westerns as: *Rachel and the Stranger* (1948); *Navajo* (1952), staring his sister-in-law Loretta Young and co-star Robert Mitchum; *Sombrero* (1953), also starring Montalban; and *Indian Paint* (1963).

In the 1950s and 1960s, Foster turned to directing and writing for television. Often these were children's films and series produced for Walt Disney, such as: *Davy Crockett; Zorro; The Nine Lives of Elfego Baca* (1958); and *Hans Brinker or the Silver Skates* (1962). Foster also directed several episodes each of such TV series as: *Adventures in Paradise* (1959); *The Loner* (1965); *Batman* (1966); *The Green Hornet* (1966); *Custer* (1967); and *It Takes a Thief* (1968).

When he died from cancer on July 7, 1976 in Santa Monica, California, Foster had directed nearly 45 films and TV shows and wrote or co-wrote either the story or the screenplay for over 20 films, all of which he directed as well. Unfortunately he never really established himself as a director of A-pictures.

Loretta Young and Sally Blane (née Elizabeth Jane Young).

Norman Foster
Actor Filmography

Gentlemen of the Press (1929)

Love at First Sight (1930)

Young Man of Manhattan (1930)

Up Pops the Devil (1931)

Under Eighteen (1931)

Reckless Living (1931)

Men Call It Love (1931)

It Pays to Advertise (1931)

Confessions of a Co-Ed (1931)

No Limit (1931)

City Streets (1931)

Week-end Marriage (1932)

Strange Justice (1932)

Skyscraper Souls (1932)

Prosperity (1932)

Play Girl (1932)

Girl of the Rio (1932)

The Cohens and Kellys in Hollywood (1932)

Alias the Doctor (1932)

Steady Company (1932)

Walls of Gold (1933)

State Fair (1933)

Rafter Romance (1933)

Pilgrimage (1933)

Professional Sweetheart (1933)

Strictly Dynamite (1934)

Orient Express (1934)

Elinor Norton (1934)

Behind the Evidence (1934)

Superspeed (1935)

Suicide Squad (1935)

The Fire Trap (1935)

Escape from Devil's Island (1935)
The Bishop Misbehaves (1935)
Behind the Green Lights (1935)
The Hoosier Schoolmaster (1935)
Ladies Crave Excitement (1935)
The Leavenworth Case (1936)
I Cover Chinatown (1936)
High Tension (1936)
Fatal Lady (1936)
Everybody's Old Man (1936)
Sunday Night at the Trocadero (1937)
Herzog Blaubarts Burg (1964)
Die Lustigen Weiber von Windsor (1965)
Play It As It Lays (1972)
A Special Act of Love (1973) (TV)
Double Solitaire (1974) (TV)

Writer/Scenarist Filmography

Fair Warning (1937)
Think Fast, Mr. Moto (1937)
Thank You, Mr. Moto (1937)
Mr. Moto Takes a Chance (1938)
Mysterious Mr. Moto (1938)
Mr. Moto's Last Warning (1939)
Mr. Moto Takes a Vacation (1939)
La Fuga (1943)
La Casa Embrujada (1944)
La Hora de la Verdad (1945)
El Ahijado de la Muerte (1946)
El Canto de la Sirena (1948)
Woman on the Run (1950)
Navajo (1952)
Sky Full of Moon (1952)

Sombrero (1953)

Davy Crockett and the River Pirates (1956)

The Nine Lives of Elfego Baca (1958)

The Sign of Zorro (1960)

Indian Paint (1963)

Die Lustigen Weiber von Windsor (1965)

Brighty of the Grand Canyon (1967)

Director Filmography

I Cover Chinatown (1936)

Fair Warning (1937)

Think Fast, Mr. Moto (1937)

Thank You, Mr. Moto (1937)

Walking Down Broadway (1938)

Mr. Moto Takes a Chance (1938)

Mysterious Mr. Moto (1938)

Charlie Chan in Reno (1939)

Mr. Moto's Last Warning (1939)

Mr. Moto Takes a Vacation (1939)

Charlie Chan at Treasure Island (1939)

Charlie Chan in Panama (1940)

Viva Cisco Kid (1940)

Ride, Kelly, Ride (1941)

Scotland Yard (1941)

Journey Into Fear (1942)

Santa (1943)

La Fuga (1943)

La Hora de la Verdad (1945)

El Ahijado de la Muerte (1946)

El Canto de la Sirena (1948)

Rachel and the Stranger (1948)

Kiss the Blood Off My Hands (1948)

Tell It to the Judge (1949)

Woman on the Run (1950)

Father Is a Bachelor (1950)

Navajo (1952)

Sky Full of Moon (1952)

Sombrero (1953)

Davy Crockett, King of the Wild Frontier (1955)

Davy Crockett and the River Pirates (1956)

"Zorro" (1957) TV Series

The Nine Lives of Elfego Baca (1958) (TV)

"Adventures in Paradise" (1959) TV Series

The Sign of Zorro (1960) (from the TV series)

Hans Brinker or the Silver Skates (1962)

Indian Paint (1963)

"The Loner" (1965) TV Series

"Batman" (1966) TV Series

"The Green Hornet" (1966) TV Series

Brighty of the Grand Canyon (1967)

"Custer" (1967) TV Series

"It Takes a Thief" (1968) TV Series

The Deathbed Virgin (1974)

Mr. Moto —
A Character Sketch

Who is Mr. Moto? Like the many fictional detectives of the time, writer John P. Marquand probably thought that his Mr. Moto character would be more interesting if his readers knew very little about him. Author Michael Pitts describes him as "much of a mystery man as some of the cases he had to solve." Throughout Marquand's novels, the eight films in the series starring Peter Lorre and the encore with Henry Silva, some clues nevertheless become apparent. The *Mr. Moto* character of Marquand's novels reveals many clues that are not mentioned in the films. Conversely, some facts from the films are never mentioned in the novels.

The inspiration for the *Mr. Moto* character came during Marquand's trip to China and Japan in the mid-1930s to gather information for a future novel. While in Japan, Marquand noticed a polite detective following him everywhere. This was probably because Japan, now starting to emerge as a military power and controlling parts of China, may have been cautious of foreigners.

In Marquand's novels, Mr. Moto is described as a polite, short, chunky man with his hair "cut after the Prussian fashion." His face is almost placid with high cheekbones, a narrow jaw, and has narrow, dark, eager eyes set behind heavy glasses. He has an uneven set of teeth shining with gold work. Moto has a preference for well-fitting European clothes. When speaking, Moto has the habit of "drawing his breath with a soft, sibilant hiss" and often says, "I am very, very sorry." His mannerisms tend to have him underestimated by his adversaries.

The reader is told virtually nothing of his family except that he is a "scion of Japanese nobility" and that his father was a diplomat in New York. The reader is not given much about the chronology of Moto's upbringing either, but Marquand does inform the reader that Moto spent some time in America. There he studied at an American university, does not speak English so well, and had been a valet for a year. Moto virtually claims to be a virtual *wunderkind*, proudly saying, "I can do many, many things. I can mix drinks and wait on table, and I am a very good valet. I can navigate and manage small boats. I have studied at two foreign universities. I also know carpentry and surveying and know five Chinese dialects." Moto however admits to at least one failing in that he "consumes whiskey like a man who had no faith in his alcoholic capacity." He therefore is

Peter Lorre as Mr. Moto

prone to taking small, careful sips.

Only the first two *Mr. Moto* films—*Think Fast, Mr. Moto* and *Thank You, Mr. Moto*—were based in any part on Marquand's novels. For the remaining six films of the series, not counting *The Return of Mr. Moto*, Norman Foster and the other writers and scenarists developed the *Mr. Moto* character in their own image, much of it remaining an enigma that viewers were required to accept at face value.

When comparing the Mr. Moto character of the novels and films, there are several similarities. Peter Lorre, the diminutive Hungarian with the moon-shaped face, portrays Mr. Moto for the first eight films. Moto is a polite man, wearing his trademarked steel-rimmed glasses, often dressed in white suits with white shoes and gloves. He goes from case to case with little facial expressions and behind his quiet *façade*, Mr. Moto can be a human mechanism of destruction using ju-jitsu who often coldly kills his attackers without remorse. He is a master of slight-of-hand, is well-read, scholarly, and besides his native Japanese, speaks English, German, and Chinese. He also has a fondness for milk and cats.

In the films, he is thought more of as a spy or secret agent rather than as a detective. Unlike many of the contemporary film detectives to which he often associated with, Mr. Moto uses disguises as part of his undercover work—a caravan camel herder, street peddler, ancient guru, escaped murderer, antique dealer, archeologist, and artist. In *Thank You, Mr. Moto*, he is described as a mysterious adventurer, explorer and soldier of fortune. Because of Lorre's small stature however, the viewer easily sees through the makeup and is not fooled.

Whatever clues one obtains from either Marquand's novels or the film series, Marquand himself gives his readers one of the greatest mysteries of them all—the character's name. The Japanese agent always introduces himself formally as "Mr. Moto" without any first name, an intentional omission similar to television's Lt. Columbo portrayed by Peter Falk. For his novels, Marquand gives his central character the unusual name, at least for a Japanese, of "I. A. Moto" without ever explaining what the initials "I. A." stand for. In the films however, Moto several times shows identification giving his name as "Kentaro Moto."

Richard Wires in his book, *John P. Marquand and Mr. Moto: Spy Adventures and Detective Films*, contends that Marquand errs in using the fictitious "Moto" family name. Although wanting to keep a simple Japanese-sounding name which is easy to remember, Wires, with the assistance of a Japanese colleague, makes the case that "Moto"—its meaning varies according to context and how it is combined—does not, or cannot stand alone as a family name. Instead, it is used as either the first element (e.g. Motogawa, Motohashi) or the final element (e.g. Anjinomoto, Yamamoto) of Japanese family names. Today however, one does find ethnic Japanese living in America having the family name of "Moto"—probably owing to their anglicizing their family name just many other ethnic groups have done.

Another area of mystery is *what is* Mr. Moto? Most books group the Mr. Moto series with others of the B-detectives of Hollywood's golden era of the 1930s and 1940s. However Mr. Moto shows very few skills that would be associated with a detective—as is best borne out in *Mr. Moto's Gamble*. Another book, *The Great Spy Pictures*, paints Moto as a secret agent but only lists a single film, *Mr. Moto's Last Warning*, as an example.

In Marquand's novels, the reader is led to believe that Mr. Moto is a fearless government agent employed in the service of the Japanese Emperor—". . . so honored to represent the interests of my Government." Also Moto says, "A servant of the Emperor is not afraid of death. It is a glory to him when he serves his Emperor." In many of the nine films, Mr. Moto identifies himself as working for the International Police—assumed to be the present-day Interpol.[14]

---

14   Interpol is the acronym for the International Criminal Police Organization, a worldwide clearinghouse for police information. Conceived in 1914, Interpol was formally established in 1923 with headquarters at Vienna but it was effectively disbanded in 1938 by Hitler's Anschluss of Austria.

After World War II, the agency was reconstituted with headquarters in Paris in 1946. Its principal services are to provide member nations (now more than 177) with information on the whereabouts of international criminals, to organize seminars on scientific crime detection, and to facilitate the apprehension of criminals, although it does not apprehend criminals directly. Interpol avoids those crimes that deal with political, military, religious, or racial matters

When defining the *Mr. Moto* character, comparisons with the inscrutable Chinese detective, Charlie Chan, cannot be avoided. To be fair, the *Charlie Chan* series of talkies from 1931 to 1947 has 44 films in which to fully develop its main character. Despite the difference in the longevity of the two series, a number of comparisons and contrasts can be made. Wires takes the position that both series relied on the premise that Orientals and mysterious events somehow went together. Warner Oland, who played Charlie Chan in 16 films from 1931 to 1938, had previously portrayed the evil Fu Manchu, while Peter Lorre had launched his movie career with his portrayal of a psychopathic child murderer in *M*.

Both Chan and Moto are shrewd, polite, wise, and intelligent—qualities that set the pair far apart from the stereotype of Hollywood's B-detectives—and both at times are permitted to use twisted humor. Both rarely drink liquor. Both are never romantically involved—Chan is married with a wife back home in Honolulu and a brood of up to 14 children while the viewer is kept in the dark on matters of Moto's family and his personal life. In fact, Moto quips in *Think Fast, Mr. Moto* that "A beautiful girl is only confusing to a man." Finally, The most notable feature of the *Charlie Chan* films is Chan's generous use of wise sayings while Moto is more restrained.

With apologies to *Charlie Chan* fans, Moto nonetheless comes off as a better character on film than his Chinese counterpart. Mr. Moto is the more physically active—albeit with a stunt double—with fist fights, use of ju-jitsu, climbing of buildings, and on-foot escapes, while the rotund Charlie Chan usually allows others to provide the needed physical dirty work. Somewhat like James Bond, Moto often kills his attackers with cold precision, while Chan rarely shoots his gun. When he does, he only wounds the assailant. Where Chan seldom uses aliases or disguises, Moto frequently relies on them in his undercover work. In *Mr. Moto Takes a Vacation*, he states that his aversion is beards despite his often using them.

---

but has been most successful with regard to counterfeiting, forgery, smuggling, and the narcotics trade.

Charlie Chan's employer is often known—be it the Honolulu Police, the U.S. Government, or his role as a private detective—it is seldom clear for whom Moto really works. Perhaps it is the International Police. In the first two films, he refers to himself as an importer. When asked in the film *Think Fast, Mr. Moto* if he is a detective, he replies that it done only as a hobby. On other occasions Moto claims to be a confidential investigator

In the best disguise of the Mr. Moto series, Peter Lorre impersonates an elderly guru in *Mr. Moto Takes a Chance*.

for the International Association of Importers, a member of the International Police, a college lecturer in criminology, and a managing director of the Dai Nippon Trading Company. All of these probably serves as a front for his activities with the International Police. However, in *The Return of Mr. Moto*, it is clear that Moto works for Interpol.

The many disguises of Mr. Moto. Clockwise from upper left: a carpet peddler (*Think Fast, Mr. Moto*); a camel herder (*Thank You, Mr. Moto*); houseboy Ito Matsuka (*Mysterious Mr. Moto*); and archeologist Professor Heinrich von Kleinroth (*Mr. Moto Takes a Vacation*).

The Mr. Moto Film Guide

The *Mr. Moto* series spans nine films—the first eight stars Peter Lorre from 1937 to 1939, and the last entry, twenty-six years later in 1965, with Henry Silva. Not all the films were released in the same order they were produced. However, the following pages represent a complete film guide to the nine films in chronological order of their release.

For each film, information about cast and crew lists, running times, release dates, etc., were primarily obtained from the *American Film Institute Catalog of Motion Pictures Produced in the United States*, onscreen credits, sources contemporaneous to the film's production, and later dated sources. Release dates are assumed to be national release dates as determined from studio records or release charts of *The Motion Picture Herald*. In the cast lists, brackets are sometimes placed around portions of certain onscreen credits. If, for example, a character's name in the onscreen credits was simply "Connie" but the film states a full name or professional title, i.e., Connie Porter, the credit will appear as Connie [Porter]. Most of the films produced after 1934 have a Production Code Administration (PCA) certification number (a.k.a. the "Hays Office") listed. These numbers were issued to films that adhered to standards of the Motion Picture Production Code. Also included are detailed storylines, notable facts, trivia, commentaries, posters, and pictures.

Only the first two films are based on any of the six *Mr. Moto* novels written by John P. Marquand. Even then, these two are only considered "adaptations" as they were extensively rewritten in terms of their characters and plots. Nevertheless, a great deal of continuity exists throughout the series in terms of the production crew and cast. Norman Foster was the director and had a role in writing either the story or the screenplay for six of the films. Besides producer Sol M. Wurtzel, who had responsibility for seven of the films, the series often utilized many of the studio's most talented crew members. Among these with three or more are: music director Samuel Kaylin, costumer Herschel McCoy, art directors Bernard Herzbraun and Lewis Creber, set decorator Thomas Little, cinematographer

Virgil Miller, sound editors Bernard Freericks and William H. Anderson, film editor Norman Colbert, and assistant director Jasper Blystone.

As producer, Sol Wurtzel showed that nepotism was alive and well at Twentieth Century-Fox, at least for the *Mr. Moto* series, as three other members of the Wurtzel family (Ben, Sam, and Dan) were also on the payroll. As for the cast, with the exception of Peter Lorre, eight actors and actresses had three appearances while 29 had two appearances. These are listed in Appendix C.

I have judged how the nine films rate on a one- to four-star rating system as follows:

Think Fast, Mr. Moto (1937)	****
Thank You, Mr. Moto (1937)	****
Mr. Moto's Gamble (1938)	**
Mr. Moto Takes a Chance (1938)	**
Mysterious Mr. Moto (1938)	***
Mr. Moto's Last Warning (1939)	**
Mr. Moto in Danger Island (1939)	*
Mr. Moto Takes a Vacation (1939)	**
The Return of Mr. Moto (1965)	*

Think Fast, Mr. Moto (1937)

Twentieth Century-Fox Film Corp. Distributed by Twentieth Century-Fox Film Corp. Released: August 27, 1937. Production: early February to early March 1937. Copyright Twentieth Century-Fox Film Corp., August 27, 1937; LP7440. Sound: Western Electric Mirrophonic Sound System. Black & White. 5,961 feet. 66 or 71 minutes. PCA certificate number 3199.

Executive producer: Sol M. Wurtzel. Director: Norman Foster. Screen play: Howard Ellis Smith and Norman Foster, based on a story by J. P. Marquand. Photography: Harry Jackson, A.S.C. Art direction: Lewis Creber. Assistant director: Solly Wurtzel, Sol Michaels,* and Tom Dudley.* Film editor: Alex Troffey. Costumes: Herschel. Sound: George Leverett and Harry M. Leonard. Musical direction: Samuel Kaylin. Dialog director: George Wright.* Revisions and additional dialog: Willis Cooper.* Contributing writer: Charles Kenyon.* Camera operator: Johnny Schmitz.* Assistant cameramen: Eddie Collins* and Tom Dowling.* Processing: Sol Halprin* and Joe Farley.* Set dresser: Walter Scott.* Wardrobe man: Sam Benson.* Wardrobe woman: Adele Farnum.* Cableman: Hal Lombard.* Boom man: Jim Burnette.* Hair stylist: Babe Carey.* Makeup: Ray Romero.* Production manager: Edward Ebele.* Grip: Al Thayer.* Assistant grip: J. Van Antwerp.* Props: Duke Abrahams.* Best boy: Ferdinand Meine.* Gaffer: Lou Johnson.* Script clerk: Jack Vernon.* Unit manager: Sam Wurtzel.* Assistant prop man: Aaron Wolf.* Still photographer: Ray Nolan.* Stunts, stand-in and double for Peter Lorre: John Kascier.* Stand-ins: Beulah Hutton* and Charlie Carroll.*

Song: *The Shy Violet* words and music by Sidney Clare and Harry Akst.

Source: Based on the story *Think Fast, Mr. Moto* (1936) by J. P. Marquand.

Cast

Peter Lorre as . . . . Mr. [Kentaro] Moto
Virginia Field . . . . Gloria Danton [alias Tanya Boriv]
Thomas Beck . . . . Bob Hitchings
Sig Rumann . . . . Nicolas Marloff
Murray Kinnell . . . . Joseph Wilkie
John Rogers . . . . Carson
Lotus Long . . . . Lela Liu
George Coopers . . . . Muggs Blake
J. Carrol Naish . . . . Adram
Fredrick Vogeding . . . . Curio dealer
George Hassell* . . . . Mr. Hitchings
Sam Tong* . . . . Chee
Tom Ung* . . . . Scar-faced man
Ray Hendricks* . . . . Soloist
Howard Wilson* . . . . Jack
Charles Irwin* . . . . Ship steward
Virginia Sale* . . . . Ship stewardess
Tom Herbert,* Isabel La Mal* . . . . Husband and wife tourists
Frank Mayo* . . . . Ship's officer
Lee Phelps* . . . . Detective
Bert Roach* . . . . Ship's bartender
Dick Alexander* . . . . Ivan
Sam Labrador* . . . . Menial
Paul Fung* . . . . Chauffeur
Soo Yong* . . . . Police telephone operator
William Law* . . . . Chief of police
Charles Tannen* . . . . unnamed

---

*Unbilled

"Love is very tiresome for a third party."
—Mr. Moto to Bob Hitchings

The Story

During celebration of the Chinese New Year's in San Francisco's Chinatown, Mr. Moto is first seen disguised as a street peddler. He carefully stares at a rug with a design of a tiger that hangs in the window of a curio shop and a man in costume with a British Union Jack tattoo on his right wrist emerges from the shop whose door has a "closed" sign. Disregarding the sign, Moto enters the shop and inquires about the rug that bears the design of the tiger but the shop owner (Fredrick Vogeding) says it is not for sale. Moto counters by offering some of his "treasures" for sale but the curio dealer declines, saying that treasures are not sold by common street peddlers as "they have no proper setting," a remark that seems so out of place that Moto takes it as some sort of recognition code. However, Moto still presses on, offering to sell the store owner a large diamond he recently acquired. He asks $5,000 claiming that the stone is easily worth $20,000 but the store owner counters with a $2,000 offer.

Moto intentionally drops the head of a carving of Kwan Yin to the floor, and when bending down to pick it up, notices a limp hand protruding from a wicker basket on the floor under the counter. He then gets up to resume haggling with the curio dealer, and just as they agree on a final price of $4,000, a police detective (Lee Phelps) notices the shop door is unlocked, enters to see if anything is amiss, and recognizes Moto as one he warned earlier in the evening for peddling without a license. Before the policeman can arrest him however, Moto quickly snatches the diamond, fights off both the policeman and shop owner, and manages to escape into the festive crowd outside the shop.

Moto safely makes his way back to his apartment and removes his disguise. The viewer first sees the moon-shaped face and protruding eyes of Peter Lorre, *sans* makeup, and the trademark steel-rimmed glasses of the refined Mr. Moto. Moto then calls the Hitchings Line to make a reservation on the *Marco Polo*, an ocean liner which is scheduled to leave at midnight for the Orient.

Bob Hitchings (Thomas Beck), is the son of the line's owner and provides half of the film's romantic love interest as an eligible young bachelor who likes to party and chase young, single women—a similar role he played in several earlier *Charlie Chan* films. Once aboard the *Marco Polo*, Bob is given a sendoff by several of his like-minded, party-hearty friends. Waiting in his stateroom however is his father (George Hassell), who also wants to see his son off. He says that he expects great things from his son in the Orient and is counting on him to put some new life into the import business. When Bob expresses a lack of self-confidence following recent failures, the elder Hitchings confidently reassures his son by saying, "You're a Hitchings! You're bound to make good if you try."

Before he leaves, the elder Hitchings gives his son an important and "extremely confidential" letter with instructions that the son is to personally give it to Joseph Wilkie (Murray Kinnell), the manager of the line's Shanghai office. He also warns his son that because one can't be sure who his fellow passengers are, he shouldn't leave the letter lying around in his stateroom.

Moto comes aboard the *Marco Polo* and is shown his stateroom—across from Hitchings'—by Carson (John Rogers), the ship steward. Hitchings and his friends see Moto standing in the hallway, are amused by his short stature and appearance, and try to persuade Moto to join them for a drink. Moto respectfully declines their offer but the celebrants will not take *no* for an answer. When Hitchings inquires of Moto why he is so quiet, Moto responds, "I am thinking about a proverb of my country—Half the world will spend its time laughing at the other half—and both are fools."

One of Bob's friends attempts to shake Moto's hand as a diversion to attempt a practical joke on Moto. Moto however is not fooled and the short Japanese displays his skill of ju-jitsu by throwing the man to the floor and then flipping Hitchings over the shoulder onto the bed. Bob quickly surrenders and says, "Well, serves us right. We asked for it and now we're friends."

Moto returns to his stateroom and requests Carson to adjust an air vent. As Carson reaches upward, Moto notices that on Carson's right wrist is the same Union Jack tattoo seen on the costumed man leaving the curio shop earlier that evening. Moto slyly smiles and knows now that Carson has something to do with the dead man in the curio shop and that the steward is a man to be watched.

On the voyage's first day out, Moto is on deck trying to overcome a minor bout of sea sickness and rough seas. He then notices Hitchings, whom he always refers to as "Mr. Bob," leaning against the ship's rail nursing a hangover resulting from the previous night's partying. Wishing to help, Moto suggests that he has the cure for what "you Americans call the 'jitters' this morning." They proceed to the ship's bar and Moto instructs the bartender (Bert Roach) as to the ingredients for an uninviting concoction called a "Hakadali highball." Despite its unappealing appearance and foul odor, Hitchings has his doubts about the mixture's curative powers but Moto encourages Bob to drink it, saying "It will improve the appearance of the world, I assure you."

Immediately after drinking the mixture, Hitchings gags and coughs several times and then proudly exclaims with a smile, "I think I'm going to live. That's great stuff Mr. Moto."

"I'm glad," replies the Japanese. The bartender then asks Moto what he wants to drink and Moto responds simply, "A glass of milk."

Hitchings then remarks, "Last night you were a ju-jitsu expert and now today you are old Doc Moto, prescriber of the world's greatest hangover cure. Who are *you* anyway?"

"I'm Mr. Moto, importer of Oriental goods with a hobby for magic," after which Moto impresses Hitchings and the bartender with his slight of hand and dexterity with cards.

"That's swell. What else can you do?" says Hitchings.

Moto follows with, "Do you want me to begin at the beginning? Too long. Where there's a beginning, there's an end. Let's end at the beginning. *Alpha, omega.*"

Hitchings replies, "*Alpha, omega?* In the words of Socrates . . ."

Moto interrupts, "Let each man help his brother man," while grasping Hitchings' hand in a form of a fraternal handshake.

Hitchings then proudly says, "Stanford '34," to which and Moto replies, "Stanford '21, honorary member." Bob now remembers Moto as the one who broke a pole vaulting record at Stanford, to which Moto politely replies with a smile, "Now I would only break the pole."

On its way to Shanghai, the *Marco Polo* arrives in Honolulu and the bachelor Hitchings laments to Moto that the crossing has been dull, he has not seen one good-looking single girl aboard ship, and there is no sign of one boarding. Moto then responds philosophically, "A beautiful girl is only confusing to a man."

Almost as if on cue however, Gloria Danton (Virginia Field) makes her way up the gangplank and immediately attracts Bob's attention. He is rebuffed however when he attempts to welcome her aboard by placing a lei around her neck. She responds curtly, "I beg your pardon." This retort surprises Hitchings, but Moto offers his assessment that "A beautiful girl knows how to say *no* in a few words." As the viewer soon learns, this happenstance meeting is no coincidence—a Shanghai-based smuggler named Nicolas Marloff (Sig Rumann) has intentionally placed both Gloria and Carson on the ship to keep an eye on the young Hitchings to learn his

Alpha, omega Mr. Bob," says Peter Lorre to Thomas Beck with Virginia Field looking on.

reason for traveling to Shanghai.

Gloria plays a hard-to-get woman by refusing Hitchings' gift of chilled champagne by ordering Carson to return the magnum with the message, "Tell Mister Hitchings, Jr., whose father owns the [shipping] line, that I am not in the habit of accepting gifts from strangers." Carson departs and Gloria smiles, a possible confirmation that Marloff's plan is taking shape. When Carson reports back to Hitchings with the unopened bottle and is given Gloria's message, Bob is disappointed and declares, "And I thought formalities were forgotten at sea."

Mr. Moto wisely responds, "When modern people cling to convention, there's nearly always a purpose."

Over the next few days of the voyage, Bob and Gloria are drawn closer together, and Bob tells her that he really has fallen for her. She tries to discourage Bob's premature thoughts of marriage, warning him that he knows little about her. While they walk on the ship's desk, Carson spies on them, an act which has not gone unnoticed by Mr. Moto. Inconspicuous while relaxing in a deck chair, Moto surprises the steward saying, "Enjoying the moonlight on the water, Mr. Carson? Very soothing to the nerves." Startled, Carson now becomes nervous with Mr. Moto around.

On the journey's last night, Mr. Moto, Mr. Bob, and Gloria are at the ship's bar when Bob and Gloria invite Moto to join them on deck. But Moto is polite enough to know when to leave the couple alone, declaring, "Young love is very tiresome for a third party" and that he is going to bed.

While going back to his room to retire for the evening, Moto finds Carson searching Mr. Bob's cabin. He attacks Carson and asks Carson for the envelope containing the important letter to Wilkie but Carson denies knowledge of it. Moto approaches Carson who then draws out a switchblade and brags that he knows that the little Japanese is not an importer. Moto responds that he recognizes the steward from the curio shop in San Francisco. The two men fist fight, with Moto also using his knowledge of ju-jitsu. As the action nears the ship's rail, Moto quickly lifts Carson up over his head and, without remorse, tosses Carson overboard. Walking back into Hitchings' cabin, Moto sees the valuable envelope on the floor and puts it in his coat pocket.

The next morning the *Marco Polo* docks in Shanghai and Bob is distressed to find that Gloria has left without telling him her address. Wilkie meets young Hitchings at the dock and is introduced to Mr. Moto as an importer that he met on the ship—"A nice chap," says Wilkie—and that they are fraternity brothers and went to the same university.

Once inside the young Hitchings' hotel room, Wilkie is disturbed that Hitchings is in love with a woman he doesn't know much about and he insists on finding her in Shanghai. He warns Bob that there has been an increase in attractive, White Russian women who, having escaped from Russia, are in Shanghai illegally without passports, and are desperately looking for ways to get out of China. Wilkie then assures Hitchings that he'll make sure that Bob meets girls of the "proper class" while in Shanghai.

Now remembering the important envelope given him, Wilkie looks inside the envelope but finds the paper blank and the two are puzzled by the contents. Moments later, the two men receive a telephone call from elder Hitchings who, after being told about the blank letter, informs his son that the original contents were to warn Wilkie that smugglers have been using the line's ships to bring contraband jewels and narcotics, concealed in Oriental curios, into the United States from China, and the shipping line has been subjected to a fine of $200,000. Bob's father thinks that the smugglers have men working on the *Marco Polo* and warns his son to be careful as he is probably being watched. After they hang up, Bob agrees to help Wilkie find the smugglers, but only after they search for Gloria.

Unknown to Hitchings and Wilkie, Mr. Moto is also listening in on the telephone conversation with the aid of Lela Liu (Lotus Long), who is both the hotel's telephone operator and an undercover agent for Moto. After Hitchings hangs up, Moto approaches Lela at the hotel's switchboard under the pretense of asking her for the address of a store that develops film for his camera. Pretending to give Moto a note with the store's address, Lela's note tells Moto that the "proper setting" can be found at the East India Bazaar. Moto then thanks her for the hotel's excellent telephone service and asks if she would care to have dinner that evening with a "lonely Japanese gentleman," which she accepts.

Mr. Moto goes to the East India Bazaar, a curio shop where he sees a rug with a design of a tiger that hangs in the window—identical to the one in San Francisco. Inside, Moto meets Adram (J. Carrol Naish), the store owner who is also part of Marloff's smuggling operation. Moto tells Adram that he prefers a decorative figurine—one "with a proper setting." Adram is surprised to hear this coming from a stranger and is immediately suspicious of Moto. After some cat-and-mouse conversation exchanges, Moto leaves the shop and Adram instructs a shop worker to follow Moto. Adram also telephones Marloff and cautions his worthy superior that an unknown Japanese "understands more than is beneficial."

Unaware that he is being tailed, Moto goes to the police station where he meets the chief of police (William Law) who is glad to see him again. The viewer now is led to believe that Moto is probably more than just an importer of Oriental goods when the police chef inquires if Moto is on an interesting case, and offers Moto whatever humble assistance he may require.

That night, Bob receives a note slipped under his hotel room door informing him that Gloria works as an entertainer at the International

Club. Moments later Wilkie comes to Hitchings' room and when told of the note's contents, Wilkie warns Bob that the cafe is in a dangerous area down by the waterfront, "patronized by people looking for a thrill." The young Hitchings insists on going there and Wilkie dutifully comes along so not as to incur the wrath of the elder Hitchings if anything were to happen to his son.

Mr. Moto and Lela also head for the International Club in individual rickshaws but Lela soon tells Moto that the route being taken by the rickshaws is not the way to the club. Moto is immediately suspicious of a trap, draws his gun, and orders the rickshaw operators to stop. Adram is waiting close by, and throws a dagger at Moto but misses. Moto then fires his gun, wounding Adram in the shoulder, and then orders the rickshaw operators to take him and Lela back towards the hotel. Shortly after they hurry away, Moto's rickshaw is broadsided by a chauffeur-driven car—ironically the one which Hitchings and Wilkie are riding in. Fortunately Moto is uninjured and when he tells Hitchings that he and Miss Liu are on their way to the International Club, Bob tells Mr. Moto that is also where they are headed and offers them a ride in their car.

At the club, they are just being about to be seated at a table when Gloria begins to sing her encore. After her performance, Bob goes to Gloria's dressing room and confronts her as to why she is working in a cabaret like the International Club. Gloria tells Bob that it is dangerous being here and confesses to really being Tanya Boriv, a White Russian emigrant employed by Marloff who gave her a job at the club. Being without a valid passport, Marloff forces her to travel under a false name and passport to discover Hitchings' plans. Muggs Blake (George Cooper), Marloff's henchman, overhears her confession to Hitchings from outside her dressing room, and reports what he has just heard to Marloff.

The two are then surprised by Marloff entering Gloria's room and he takes them both as prisoners into a vault located in the basement's private gambling room—which also serves as the focal point for his smuggling activities. Marloff then goes out to the dance floor to the table where Mr. Moto, Lela Liu, and Wilkie are seated. Moto is showing his skill at stacking wooden matchsticks, to which Lela remarks, "I don't know how you keep from spoiling it."

"Patience, my dear Miss Liu, is the most useful of virtues," Moto replies.

Marloff greets everyone and addresses Wilkie by name, startling the shipping representative who questions how Marloff knows his name since they have never met before. Marloff responds that he recognized Wilkie from having seen him many times around town.

Moto inquires about gambling, and Marloff tells him that he can supply almost any game and has a gambling room in the basement for this very purpose. Wilkie, on the other hand declines Marloff's offer to join Moto as he confesses, "I never indulge in games of chance."

Moto counters, "You should try it, Mr. Wilkie. I find it very exhilarating."

Under the guise of writing a *haiku* verse, Mr. Moto really writes a message in Japanese to Lela for her to call the police for help after he leaves the table for the gambling room. However, she is shot while inside a telephone booth by an unknown assailant just as she tells the police that she is calling for Mr. Moto at the International Club.

Once inside the gambling room, Mr. Moto tells Marloff that he is very much interested in a tiger symbol on the wall and notes that he has seen a similar one in a San Francisco curio shop just off Grant Avenue. Moto then states, "Certainly your establishment appears profitable. On the other hand, it is possible that business alone is not enough. If one had a sideline . . ."

Mr. Moto proceeds to tell Marloff that he is a smuggler too and suggests they join forces in an equal partnership for their own protection and profit. He further assures Marloff that he knows what happens to those who try to deceive him, citing the fate of the man stuffed into a wicker crate in the San Francisco curio shop. Marloff still probes further, asking what Moto's connection is with Bob Hitchings.

Moto inquires about the whereabouts of Bob and Gloria, and Muggs shows them bound and gagged in the vault. When Marloff tells Moto that he plans to have Hitchings dumped in the river while taking Gloria with him, Mr. Moto reminds Marloff that Hitchings' father is wealthy and may be worth more alive than dead. As for Gloria, Moto suggests that she be killed as a traitor.

Looking for what has become of Hitchings and Moto, Wilkie wanders down to the basement and asks where the gambling room is. He is told that it is closed but nonetheless knocks on the door and is let in. Inside, Wilkie sees Hitchings tied and demands his release at once. When his gag is removed, Hitchings warns Wilkie that Moto is a crook and is "in with Marloff."

Suddenly, the wounded Adram enters the gambling room through a rear door. He sees Moto and warns Marloff that Moto is a police spy—the man who shot him—and is the man he had followed to the police station. Moto draws his gun and Wilkie, apparently by accident, bumps Moto's gun hand, causing Moto to shoot himself in the stomach. Marloff kneels over, taunting Moto. "Now think fast, Mr. Moto. So, *you're* a police spy."

Apparently near death, Mr. Moto requests that Marloff use a gun to deliver a merciful *coup de grâce*. Just as Marloff is about to finish Moto off, Moto reaches for Marloff and flips him away. Adram begins to draw his gun and Moto shoots the assailant. Getting up and apparently unharmed, Mr. Moto requests that Wilkie retrieve Marloff's gun inside Marloff's dinner jacket. As Wilkie reaches inside, the gun discharges, killing Marloff instantly.

Wilkie apologizes for the gun firing prematurely, to which Moto replies without emotion, "That would seem to dispose of Mr. Marloff." The chief of police and his reinforcements now enter the gambling room and Hitchings, seeing that the police chief knows Moto, then apologizes to him, admits he was fooled, and thanks Moto for saving their lives.

Wilkie also comes forward to apologize and to congratulate Moto. Quickly, Moto then handcuffs Wilkie. Hitchings is astounded and asks, "Who are you anyway?"

The little Japanese produces a business card identifying himself as Kentaro Moto, the managing director of the Dai Nippon Trading Company. "You've heard of us?" asks Mr. Moto, to which Hitchings replies, "Of course, you're our best customer. But I don't understand . . ."

"My business, as well as yours, was being seriously jeopardized by the smuggling activities of Mr. Marloff and his friends," says Moto.

"Oh, then you're not a detective after all?" asks Hitchings.

"Oh, only as a hobby." Moto further explains that it was not an accident that Wilkie shot Marloff. From the elder Hitchings' letter to Mr. Wilkie, Moto tells that he had long suspected that someone in Wilkie's position was in charge of the smuggling. Furthermore, Moto points out that since Marloff earlier made the unfortunate mistake by recognizing Wilkie in the club upstairs, that Wilkie had found the gambling room and gained entrance by knowing the correct knocking sequence, he was practically certain of Wilkie's role. Despite all of this, Mr. Moto wants even stronger proof—he gives Wilkie the opportunity to kill the only man who knows that he is the head of the smuggling ring. The "smoking " gun, including a silencer, is found in Wilkie's pocket when searched by the police at Moto's request. Moto is then told that Lela was shot, but is now recovering.

The final mystery as to the secret of Moto's miraculous recovery from being shot is now solved—Mr. Moto reveals a bullet-proof vest underneath his dinner jacket which stopped the bullet. Hitchings now correctly concludes that is was Moto who slipped the note under his hotel door as part of his plan to bring Wilkie to the club. "*Alpha, omega* Mr. Bob," says Moto with a toothy smile and congratulatory fraternal handshake.

"*Alpha, omega*" is the refrain echoed by Bob and Gloria.

Commentary

Of all the films in the *Mr. Moto* series, *Think Fast, Mr. Moto* probably ranks second behind *Thank You, Mr. Moto* in quality. Some of the mystery of the film, and of the series as a whole, centers on who or what *is* Mr. Moto as there seems to be no consensus of opinion. Is he a secret agent or spy in the service of his Japanese emperor or is he a detective? When near the film's end, Bob Hitchings asks Moto who he is and the polite Japanese produces a card identifying himself as an importer and remarks that he is a detective only as a hobby. After several films in the series, the viewer probably will conclude that it is the importing business that serves as Moto's hobby.

In hindsight, it's hard to imagine anyone else fitting the *Mr. Moto* character as well as Peter Lorre does—short in stature with the round face, protruding eyes, and that oh so distinctive voice. Besides the character's trademarked steel-rimmed glasses, only false buck teeth and a minimum of makeup were needed to complete the transformation. Although Mr. Moto often uses disguises—with an aversion for beards—the viewer nonetheless is not fooled as Lorre's height and voice are instant giveaways. Despite all this, Moto's disguise does bring some entertainment to the story while he works *incognito*.

In it's review of the film, *Variety* is pleased with Lorre's new characterization as it "gets away from the grim villainy of his previous film efforts. The new Peter Lorre probably will be rated as a find by others who heretofore knew him only as a dyed-in-wool villain." Even John T. McManus of the *New York Times* in his August 16, 1937 review agreed. "Mr. Lorre is certainly the man for Mr. Marquand's Mr. Moto."

Although of Hungarian origin, the casting of Lorre in the series' first entry continued the common Hollywood practice of its studios casting non-Orientals in roles where the main character is Oriental. Previous, the *Charlie Chan* series used Warner Oland. After Lorre's Mr. Moto, Charlie Chan continued to be played by Sidney Toler and Roland Winters. Even the short-lived *Charlie Chan* television series in the late '50s had J. Carrol Naish in the featured role. Besides Chan and Moto, Boris Karloff portrayed the Chinese detective lead in the *Mr. Wong* series.

Although Norman Foster does a good job of keeping the film's pace from dragging down, his screenplay does have a few holes in it which leaves the viewer with some questions. First, after escaping from the San Francisco curio shop and returning to the relative safety of his hotel room, it is amazing that Moto, without having to open a telephone book, dials the correct telephone number of the Hitchings Line to secure a reservation on the *Marco Polo* that night. But then, the reader of Marquand's novels, not the viewer of this first entry, is already made aware that Moto is a man of many talents and abilities. Perhaps Mr. Moto, already knows this number, having looked it up earlier and possessing a good memory, is able to instantly recall it. But then, for what purpose? There is no mention why Moto wants to go to the Orient, and why the Hitchings Line? The viewer is probably left thinking that it has something to do with the earlier events at the curio shop and that he is probably already on a case.

The fight scene with Carson in Hitchings' cabin, gives the viewer its first glimpse that, despite his polite and cultured exterior and a fondness for milk, Mr. Moto is a lethal instrument of human destruction—a nimble and fearless fighter (albeit with Lorre using John Kascier as a stunt double). This skill easily sets him apart from most of the B-film detectives of the 1930s and 1940s, especially from that of both Charlie Chan and Mr. Wong who showed no athletic prowess at all.

Despite his potential to employ ruthless and deadly tactics, Moto also exhibits a lighter side. He knows when not to interfere in matters of the heart between two people. He also shows his concern for the well-being of those he considers a close acquaintance, such as offering to cure Bob Hitchings' hangover with his Hakadali highball concoction.[15]

Film Notes

Twentieth Century-Fox by 1936 already had a film series featuring an Oriental detective in its successful *Charlie Chan* series. Nevertheless, the studio tried to capitalize on the Chinese detective's popularity by acquiring the film rights of several *Mr. Moto* novels written by the future Pulitzer Prize winning author John P. Marquand to introduce another Oriental detective, a Japanese.

Marquand was a well-established contributor to the *Saturday Evening Post* when, in 1934, the magazine provided him with a trip to the Orient to gather new material for his fiction. Marquand wandered from China to Japan where a polite little Japanese detective followed him about and provided the inspiration for a series character, Mr. I. A. Moto.

Think Fast, Mr. Moto, Marquand's third novel constructed around the

---

15   The recipe is as follows: Into a tall glass add one measure of lemon juice, a pinch of salt, one egg (cracked), four dashes of orange bitters, one jigger of worcheshire sauce, two teaspoons of sugar, one pony of absinthe, full glass up with gin, and stir gently.

Mr. Moto character, became the basis for Twentieth Century-Fox's first film entry of the same name. According to company records, Marquand was paid $7,000 for the film rights to his novel prior to its serialization in the *Saturday Evening Post* in six consecutive issues from September 12 to October 17, 1936. The film's production got underway in February 1937 and was completed one month later with the official release on August 27, 1937.

The *Variety* review of August 18, 1937 for *Think Fast, Mr. Moto* presumed that ". . . Peter Lorre had been cast in the title role as a trial balloon to determine whether his screen work as an Oriental would click with audiences." The reviewer's opinion then confirmed the studio's hope that the *Mr. Moto* film would catch on as a series. In all, *Think Fast, Mr. Moto* was followed by seven more *Mr. Moto* entries starring Peter Lorre in the lead role. In 1965, Twentieth Century-Fox revised the series and produced a ninth film starring Henry Silva, *The Return of Mr. Moto*, a film that was probably better left unmade.

Neophyte director Norman Foster, who also wrote the film's screenplay with Howard Ellis Smith, was chosen by producer Sol Wurtzel to direct the initial entry as well as six of the eight films that featured Peter Lorre. Viewers already familiar with the *Charlie Chan* series will easily recognize many of Fox's stable of contract players and crew. Thomas Beck, as he did in four *Chan* films, plays the role of a young bachelor both in this film and the series' second entry, *Thank You, Mr. Moto*. Beck had appeared with Peter Lorre in *Crack-Up* (1936). Virginia Field plays the other half of the story's romantic pair in addition to appearances in two other films of the *Mr. Moto* series. Murray Kinnell, a veteran of four *Chan* films, however only appears in this initial entry. Lesser roles are portrayed by *Chan* alumni of John Rogers, Fredrick Vogeding, J. Carrol Naish, and Lee Phelps.

When compared to the novel, there are several major differences in both characterizations and plot. Wilson Hitchings of the novel now becomes Robert Hitchings, Jr. The novel presents the Hitchings Brothers as a respected American banking firm lead by Wilson's uncle William instead of the shipping line run by Hitchings' father in the film.

Much of the film's intrigue takes place aboard the *Marco Polo* on its way to Shanghai and the smuggling of jewels and drugs from the Interna-

Clockwise from the upper left: Thomas Beck, Virginia Field, J. Carrol Naish, and Murray Kinnell.

tional Club to San Francisco using the family's shipping line. Readers of the novel will recognize the connection between the Honolulu gambling activities of the Hitchings Plantation casino by cousin Eva Hitchings and the secret financing of anti-Japanese activities by Chinese and Soviet agents in the puppet state of Manchukuo (Manchuria), who apparently use the Hitchings bank as a conduit. This would be the last film for George Hassell, who played the elder Hitchings. He died on February 17, 1937 at the age of 55 just after production started on the film.

The film also has some nice cultural and historical touches although some viewers may not be aware of them. Mr. Moto shows the carving of Kwan Yin, the Buddhist goddess of mercy,[16] to the owner of the San Francisco curio shop. Moto also dabbles in the art of *haiku*.[17] The story line uses the presence of Shanghai's International Settlement to justify the presence of European residents, especially Russians.[18]

---

16   Kwan Yin evolved through the Buddhist movement to the female goddess symbolizing mercy and protection. Kwan Yin occurs again in *Thank You, Mr. Moto*.

17   Haiku is a traditional Japanese verse form expressing a single emotion or idea in which 17 syllables are arranged in three lines consisting of five, seven, and five syllables respectively. The form emerged during the 16th century and was developed into a refined medium of Buddhist and Taoist symbolism.

18   Shanghai is the Chinese city that is the central location of the film, *Think Fast, Mr. Moto*. It is one of the world's largest seaports and is a major industrial and commercial center of China. Shanghai is located on the coast of the East China Sea on the mouth of the Yangtze River to the north, and Hangchow (Hangzhou) Bay to the south. The name Shanghai, also called Hu for short in Chinese, dates from the Sung dynasty (960–1126), in which it emerged from previously being a small fishing village.
      Defeated by Great Britain in 1842, the Chinese surrendered Shanghai and signed the Treaty of Nanking, which opened the city as the first Chinese port to unrestricted foreign trade. In a series of "concessions," the British (1843), French (1849), and Americans (1862) took possession of designated foreign zones in the city in which they were granted special rights and privileges, which included their own courts, police system, and armies. In 1863, the British and Americans combined their sectors into what was called the International Settlement, which contributed to the city's strong cosmopolitan atmosphere. The Japanese also received a concession in 1895 under the terms of the Treaty of Shimonoseki. In 1943, England and the United States renounced their claims to Shanghai and as did France in 1946.

Peter
LORRE
in

THANK YOU, MR. MOTO

Thomas
BECK · **FREDERICK**
Barton

Jayne
REGAN · **BLACKMER**
Sidney

Sig
RUMANN · **CARRADINE**
John

Thank You, Mr. Moto (1937)

Twentieth Century-Fox Film Corp. Distributed by Twentieth Century-Fox Film Corp. Released: December 24, 1937. Production: late October to mid-November 1937. Copyright Twentieth Century-Fox Film Corp., December 24, 1937; LP7960. Sound: Western Electric Mirrophonic Recording. Black & White. 7 reels. 6,100 feet. 67–68 minutes. PCA certificate number 3828.

Executive producer: Sol M. Wurtzel. Director: Norman Foster. Screen play: Willis Cooper and Norman Foster, based on a story by John P. Marquand. Photography: Virgil Miller, A.S.C. Art direction: Bernard Herzbrun and Albert Hogsett. Film editors: Irene Morra and Nick DeMaggio. Costumes: Herschel. Sound: Joseph E. Aiken and William H. Anderson. Musical direction: Samuel Kaylin. Assistant Director: William Eckhardt.* Second assistant director: Jerry Braun.* Contributing writer: Jerry Cady.* Second cameraman: L. B. Abbott.* Assistant cameraman: Ted Weisbarth* and W. E. Meinardus.* Gaffer: Fred Hall.* Assistant cutter: Eleanor Morra.* Wardrobe man: John Hassett.* Wardrobe woman: Gladys Isaacson.* Assistant sound: J. Sigler.* Boom man: Harry Kornfield.* Cable man: E. J. La Valla* Hair stylist: Wilma Ryan.* Makeup: Ben Nye.* Production manager: Edward Ebele.* Unit manager: Sam Wurtzel.* Script clerk: Jack Vernon.* Grip: Rodney Murphy.* Assistant grip: Harry R. Jones.* Props: Duke Abrahams.* Assistant prop men: Ralph Hearst* and Stanley Detlie.* Best boy: John Grady.* Still photographer: Jerry Milligan.* Stunts: Jack Woody.*

Source: Based on the short story *Thank You, Mr. Moto* by J. P. Marquand (1936).

Cast

Peter Lorre *as* . . . . Mr. [Kentaro] Moto
Thomas Beck . . . . Tom Nelson
Pauline Frederick . . . . Madame Chung
Jayne Regan . . . . Eleanor Joyce
Sidney Blackmer . . . . Herr [Eric] Koerger
Sig Rumann . . . . Colonel Tchernov
John Carradine . . . . Pieriera
William Von Brincken . . . . Schneider
Nedda Harrigan . . . . Madame Tchernov
Philip Ahn . . . . Prince Chung
John Bleifer . . . . Ivan
James B. Leong* . . . . policeman

*Unbilled

"Birth is not a beginning; death is not an end."
—Mr. Moto to Tom Nelson

The Story

The opening scene finds Mr. Moto in disguise, having joined a camel caravan traveling across the vast Gobi Desert during a violent windstorm. Alone in his tent before settling down for the night, Moto examines a scroll painting and then rolls it up and inserts inside a hollow walking staff. As he prepares to go to sleep, the focus of his eyes goes around the tent as he is now suspicious of everything after a bungled attempt to kill him was made earlier that day. Ning the Mongolian caravan leader enters Moto's tent during the night with a knife. When he is about kill Moto, the Japanese agent surprises the assailant and after a brief scuffle, mercilessly stabs Ning three swift times. Moto then quickly digs a makeshift grave inside the tent to hide the body.

Days later the caravan arrives at Peiping. At a checkpoint, Moto is stopped and questioned by the police who are searching for smugglers. The inspector becomes suspicious of Moto as a camel herder, examines his staff, and breaks it in half over his knee to reveal the hidden scroll. Moto quickly grabs the scroll from the inspector's hand and leads the police on a foot chase through the streets. Moto then dashes into a loading dock entrance of the Grand Hotel and takes the freight elevator to an upper floor. Exiting the elevator, Mr. Moto knocks on an apartment door and gains entrance when opened by Wing, his Chinese servant who doesn't recognize his master. Moto deceives the pursuing police by making them think he jumped out the bathroom window to the street below and escaped.

After removing his disguise and taking a well-deserved bath, Mr. Moto dresses in a robe and slippers and relaxes in a chair with Chungkina, his cat, while catching up on his mail. In one envelope Moto finds a surprising invitation from a Colonel Tchernov requesting his attendance at a garden party being held that evening. Moto then wonders aloud, "Garden parties are seldom held in Peiping without a purpose Chungkina. I wonder what Colonel Tchernov's purpose is?"

The scene then shifts to the party at Tchernov's residence where Tchernov (Sig Rumann) is introducing members of the city's diplomatic corps to the guest of honor, Eleanor Joyce (Jayne Regan), the daughter of Norton Joyce, a well-known importer. Next in line is Tom Nelson (Thomas Beck), a code clerk with the American legation, who kisses Eleanor's hand and introduces himself with a novel pick-up line. "I been wanting to meet you Miss Joyce ever since I made an interesting discovery about you."

"What?" answers Eleanor.

"Well you see, I'm psychic," he responds. "I have been in this country just long enough to soak up some of its Oriental mysticism and last night for instance, I went into this trance and, eh, shall we dance and I'll tell you all about it?"

After Tom and Eleanor leave for the dance floor, Tchernov asks his butler Ivan (John Bleifer) if Mr. Moto has arrived yet and then turns to his partner Eric Koerger (Sidney Blackmer) wondering if Moto has been delayed for some reason.

Coincidentally, the tone of the music shifts as Moto enters the garden—his entrance has not gone unnoticed by Tchernov and Koerger. On his way to thank Colonel Tchernov for inviting him, Moto walks by Nelson, pausing to say hello, as the two apparently know each other. Eleanor asks Tom who the man is and he explains *that* man is Mr. Moto—"adventurer, explorer, soldier of fortune. One of the Orient's mysteries. Nobody knows very much about him except that when he shows up, something usually happens." Fascinated, Eleanor wants to meet Moto and Tom obliges.

Tom approaches his host and requests that Tchernov introduce Moto to Eleanor. In addressing Mr. Moto, Eleanor tries to impress him by speaking a few words of greeting in Japanese. Moto responds in kind and then offers a question. However, Eleanor is now embarrassed when she confesses that she only knows a few words in Japanese and doesn't understand his reply. Always the diplomatic gentleman though, Moto downplays the situation when he remarks that Eleanor's Japanese pronunciation is superb and that he has once met her father, praising him as a true connoisseur of Oriental art.

Nelson informs Moto that Miss Joyce is in China to pick up some antiques herself and is also writing a book on Chinese art. These facts impress Moto—he remarks that it is rare to find beauty, youth, and an appreciation for fine art in a woman. However, Mr. Moto cautions Eleanor that deception is a fine art with dealers in Oriental antiques, to which Tom jokes that he once bought a jade Buddha that turned out to be soapstone.[19]

To be sociable, Koerger asks Eleanor to dance and quips, "One meets every nationality in Peiping, even Chinese." He also points out Madame Chung (Pauline Frederick) and her son Prince Chung (Philip Ahn) as Chinese nobility, both sitting alone at a distant table. Eleanor remarks that the Chung matriarch reminds her of pictures of the empress dowager, to which

---

19   Soapstone, also called steatite, is a soft talc in rock form used in applications such as griddles, bed warmers, and thermostatic heaters.

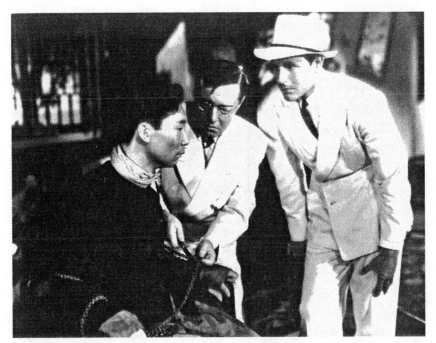

A devastated Prince Chung, portrayed by Philip Ahn, is rescued by Peter Lorre and Thomas Beck.

Koerger adds that Madame Chung was once a lady-in-waiting to the empress and that she disapproves of modern China *and* of foreigners.

As the party's host, Tchernov stops by the Chungs' table to see if they are enjoying themselves.

However his main purpose in inviting them is to discuss a matter of importance with the prince. In his library Tchernov tells Prince Chung that he wishes to purchase a few "minor" items from the Chung family treasure. Specifically Tchernov is interested in a famous set of scroll paintings that date back to the days of Kublai Khan of the Yu'an Dynasty. Chung inquires if these are for his host's own collection but Tchernov lies and says that they are for a friend. Chung complains that too few of his country's treasures are left in China, that the scrolls have been handed down through twelve generations of his family, and he cannot part with them.

Tchernov responds that he will make it worth the prince's while but Chung is now insulted and counters, "Among our people, social gatherings are *not* arranged for the purpose of transacting business deals." Tchernov says if the prince won't sell, he'll find other ways of getting the scrolls. Chung vows that his ancestors' honor is at stake and he will not sell his family's treasures at any price. Now frustrated and left with very few options, Tchernov pulls a gun on Chung and threatens that he will not leave the room until he changes his mind.

The setting immediately turns to the garden where Eleanor sees the prince leaving with his mother. Eleanor enters the library and finds Tchernov slumped over his desk with a gun in his hand. When she looks closer to see if he is dead, the body falls to the floor. She is about to telephone the police when Mr. Moto suddenly appears out from the shadows saying, "He's quite dead, I assure you. Most regrettable." Aghast, Eleanor insists that something must be done, like calling the police, but Moto removes the gun to his pocket—"There's very little the police can do about suicide."

"But it *can't* be suicide. The gun was in his hand," insists Eleanor.

However Moto turns over the body to reveal a knife protruding from Tchernov's abdomen and he positions Tchernov's hand as if it were grasping the handle. "It *is* suicide Miss Joyce. We call it *hara-kiri.* He stabbed himself, as you can see." Eleanor continues to object to Moto's explanation of the events, knowing it was murder. Mr. Moto then relents, "Of course it is murder dear lady, but it would be difficult to prove it. Would it not?"

Later at Prince Chung's home, the prince thanks Moto for saving his unworthy life when the Japanese agent stabbed Tchernov just as he was about to shoot the prince. The prince asks Mr. Moto how he can show his gratitude in some more tangible form than words. Moto requests that he would honored to see the set of scroll paintings that Colonel Tchernov was anxious to obtain. After a brief departure, the prince retrieves the scrolls from their hiding place inside a vault behind a family religious shrine and unravels the scrolls while telling Moto that an illustrious ancestor painted the scrolls many centuries ago. Although originally there are said to be seven scrolls, the prince says that his family has six scrolls and legend holds that the seventh scroll is hidden in a lamasery in the Gobi Desert.

Moto is impressed with the scrolls' beauty and now appreciates why Tchernov wanted them. The prince says that Tchernov's motives were prompted by something beyond the love of art. Chung then recounts how his father said that when placed in order, the scrolls form a picture map showing the location of an immense treasure hidden in the tomb of Genghis Khan. Moto asserts that the tomb has never been found but the prince says that Genghis Khan is buried in a forest near the edge of the Gobi Desert and the scrolls are supposed to indicate the burial place and the lost treasure—corroborative proof Moto was waiting to hear. Prince Chung is taken aback when Moto reveals he was sent to Peiping to learn if the treasure exists and was to take the necessary steps to recover it with the prince and his mother being amply rewarded. However the prince is emphatic that his family has no desire for anyone to locate the tomb and take its treasure.

Looking at the first scroll, Moto comments that the pictured bridge looks familiar. Chung identifies it as the nearby Marco Polo Bridge—the starting point of the journey. The second scroll shows a sampan sailing into the setting sun which Moto concludes that part of the journey is west-

ward up the Hun Ho river. However, the third scroll is missing and when in the middle of explaining that it contains a particular pagoda, Chung is interrupted by his mother who scolds her son for showing the scrolls to a stranger and orders him to return the scrolls to the vault. Embarrassed, Mr. Moto apologizes to the matriarch for his imposition.

Madame Chung lectures Moto about the House of Chung, quoting the family oath—"Honor above wealth, tradition above self"—recalling that many men have been searching for the tomb of Genghis Khan for over 600 years. She apologizes to Moto for appearing impolite but explains that they have already lost one of the scrolls, stolen from a local museum while on loan for an exhibition of Yu'an Dynasty art.

Although the Chungs posted a reward for the scroll's return, the only response was from a shady antique dealer who pretended he had made a mistake as soon as he discovered that the Chungs were the real owners.

On the day after the murder, Tom Nelson stops by Tchernov's house to pick up Miss Joyce to go shopping. In the library Eleanor is being shown Chinese antiques for sale by Pieriera (John Carradine), a crooked antique dealer. He shows her a statuette of Kwan Yin from the T'ang Dynasty and a jade Buddha from the Wei Dynasty. However it is a scroll painting that catches her eye but Pieriera asks too much for it—$2,000. He doesn't make the sale but he gives her his card and invites her to visit his shop to look around.

Unknown to Moto, he is being watched by Schneider (William Von Brincken), a henchman of Tchernov and Koerger. Mr. Moto enters Pieriera's shop and tells the dealer that he is looking for a scroll painting from the Yu'an Dynasty, but Pieriera says that these are rare and very expensive. Nevertheless, Moto says he is prepared to pay if he finds one that matches a famous set. Pieiera indicates he has one from the 13th century and while he leaves the room to get the scroll, Moto picks up a *samisen* on display and plays a few notes as he hums a tune.

By this time Pieriera returns and praises Moto on his expertise with the instrument. He then shows Moto a scroll and describes it as "very ancient" and asks $2,000. However, Moto's inspection tells him the scroll is not 13th century but is a recent fake. Taken aback, Pieriera gives the excuse that he bought the scroll from a coolie who stole it from a temple. However Mr. Moto doesn't believe him and claims Pieriera stole the real Chung-Yu'an scroll from the museum. Moto wants to know who paid him to steal it. Pieriera is now frightened and declares that he will be killed if he talks. Moto increases the verbal pressure further and just when Pieriera is about to give the name, he is shot dead by Schneider from a passing car but who instead was trying to kill Moto. In the confusion from the crowd and police that gather outside after hearing the shots, Moto grabs the fake scroll and escapes.

Mr. Moto returns to his hotel room and finds its contents ransacked. However the actions of his cat tell his master someone hiding in the room behind a curtain. As a ruse to flush out the intruder, Moto telephones the hotel manager, saying that he wishes to place a valuable art treasure in the hotel's safe. He leaves his gun, which he purposely loaded with blanks, on a

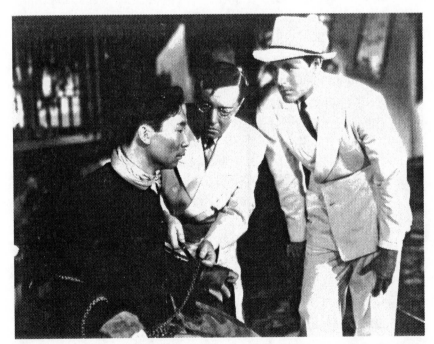

In action reminiscent from *The Wizard of Oz*, Peter Lorre, Philip Ahn, Norman Foster, Pauline Frederick, and Thomas Beck take a stroll during a break in filming *Thank You, Mr. Moto*.

table before he enters the bathroom. The gun is then quickly picked up by Schneider who had been hiding in the room. While in the bathroom, Moto checks to see if the real Chung-Yu'an scroll which he brought back from the Gobi Desert is still safe—hidden in the cleanout trap of a sewer pipe. Satisfied, he then carries the fake scroll he took from Pieriera's shop into the living room where he is now met by Schneider who demands the scroll and Moto obliges. When Moto makes a sudden move as to escape, Schneider fires Moto's gun and Moto falls to the floor.

After Schneider leaves, Moto gets up, grabs his gun replacing blanks with real bullets, and follows Schneider to Tchernov's home. Inside the house, Ivan tells Eleanor that Madame Tchernov (Nedda Harrigan) had retired early and Eleanor goes to the house library to find a suitable book for reading. She starts to retrieve a book about Genghis Khan when she sees Madame Tchernov dressed with an overcoat and hat entering the library, where she opens a hidden safe and removes a scroll. The recent widow then picks up the telephone, asks the operator to dial a number, and then talks to someone she calls "darling" with the message that she has the scroll and she is now leaving to join him.

After Eleanor sees Madame Tchernov leave in Schneider's car, she returns to the library where she meets Mr. Moto trying to break into the safe. To his disappointment, Moto is told that Madame Tchernov already took the scroll from the safe. Moto reveals to Eleanor that they both are interested in scrolls but Eleanor, referring to Moto's stabbing of Colonel Tchernov earlier, remarks that she didn't kill anyone to get one. Unabashed and with a straight face, Moto replies, "Of course. I thought it was a very good reason."

Moto stops Eleanor from telephoning the police a second time and reveals that he is really a confidential detective for the International Association of Importers, but only as a hobby which under the present circumstances, allows him to combine it with his profession of an importer. With help from the telephone company and Eleanor, Moto traces the owner of the telephone number that Madame Tchernov called earlier and now calls Prince Chung's house. Moto speaks in Chinese to Koerger, who is now impersonating the prince, to warn him of an attempt to steal the scrolls that evening. However, Moto is not fooled by Koerger's impersonation and now fears the prince and his mother are in danger. Mr. Moto suggests that Eleanor tell Tom to come over to stay with her as a precaution. As he is about to leave, Moto is knocked unconscious by Ivan who was listening to the events from the hallway. Ivan then forces Miss Joyce to go with him to meet Koerger later.

At Prince Chung's house, Koerger and Schneider tear the house apart to look for the remaining scrolls. Not finding them, Koerger nonetheless insists that the scrolls have to be in the house somewhere and reminds Schneider that Moto telephoned the prince to warn him. But Schneider says that the caller couldn't have been Moto as he is dead, as he had shot Moto earlier to get the scroll Moto brought back from the Gobi desert. Koerger reminds Schneider that he also thought he killed Moto in Pieriera's shop. Irritated, Koerger had previously warned Schneider not to underestimate Moto. Madame Tchernov adds that if Moto is so clever, he may have not been fooled by Koerger's impersonation of the prince either and may have already called the police.

Still not finding the scrolls and wasting valuable time, Koerger and Schneider then torture Prince Chung, who is bound in a chair but refuses to reveal the hiding place of the scrolls. Getting nowhere with the prince alone, Koerger has Schneider bring Madame Chung into the room and Koerger strikes her to force her son to give up his silence. Helpless to do anything himself, the prince now can't bear to see his mother beaten anymore and finally tells Koerger the location of the scrolls. The thieves, thinking they now have all seven scrolls, are about to leave when Madame Chung tries to attack Schneider with a knife but Koerger shoots and kills her.

Meanwhile, Tom Nelson arrives at Tchernov's house to be with Eleanor but finds the front door open and Mr. Moto unconscious on the floor. Nelson finally arouses Moto who says that Eleanor was probably taken to Prince Chung's house—where Moto and Nelson now are headed.

They finally arrive at Prince Chung's house and untie the prince but cannot do anything for his slain mother. Devastated, and believing that he has shamed his ancestors, Prince Chung grabs the knife from the floor, kneels before the family shrine, and commits suicide by stabbing himself. Moto and Tom rush to the prince's side and before the prince dies, he confesses that he has brought dishonor on his family and has betrayed the secret of the tomb of Genghis Khan. Moto promises Chung that he will avenge the death of his mother and that no one shall desecrate the tomb.

Koerger, Schneider, Ivan, and Madame Tchernov with Miss Joyce as their hostage, drive towards the city gates, telling the police guard that they are taking a trip out of the city for the weekend. Once outside Peiping, they head to the Marco Polo Bridge where they have a junk waiting to take them on the rest of their journey to find the lost treasure. Close behind in a speeding car are Moto and Tom Nelson. When they reach the city gate, Moto shouts to the guard, "I am Mr. Moto, International Police," and tells the guard to contact the marshal of Peiping to apprehend Koerger and his gang. Moto fears if they don't stop the thieves before they reach the river, they will never find Eleanor.

When Tom's car approaches the place where Koerger's junk is docked, he drives the car over the bank into the water to avoid being shot at. Tom climbs out from the water but is immediately captured by the gang. Still in the water, Mr. Moto fools the thieves that he has drowned after being apparently shot by Schneider. Aboard the junk, Tom tells Koerger that Moto told the police to follow them but Koerger doubts they will be successful adding, "The route we're taking hasn't been discovered for 600 years."

Mr. Moto secretly climbs onboard the junk, tosses Ivan overboard, and knocks out Schneider before entering the cabin to confront Koerger. With confidence, Moto cautions Koerger not to shoot him as Moto reveals that the scroll he allowed Schneider to take from his room is only an imitation and he has the real one safely hidden away. "If you shoot me, we shall both regret it. I assure you," he warns. Moto then tells Koerger that he knows the Mongolian in the Gobi Desert was sent to kill him and capture the scroll. The two sides realize that they need each other as one can not do anything without the other. As a compromise Moto suggests that they join forces as the treasure is enough for all of them.

Madame Tchernov begins carping with Koerger, her lover, complaining that Moto is stalling for time and that Koerger is foolish to trust Moto. Seeing an opportunity to drive a wedge between Madame Tchernov and Koerger by pitting one against the other, Moto declares, "Madame Tchernov, it is unwise to trust anyone—even a lady with your suspicious nature can sometimes be deceived." Moto plays heavily on Madame Tchernov's jealousy of Eleanor and convinces the widow that Koerger planned to get rid of her in favor of Eleanor after obtaining all the scrolls. Eleanor joins in the deception when she speaks to Tom who is now confused by the events, "Can't you see through Tom, the way I was using you to fool Madame Tchernov?"

Now upset, Madame Tchernov starts an argument with Koerger and accidentally grabs Koerger's gun hand, shooting Schneider dead. In a dramatic fight scene with Koerger that follows, Mr. Moto fatally shoots Koerger. Moto then politely bows towards Madame Tchernov saying, "I am so grateful for your suspicious nature. It is the not the first time a woman's jealousy has been fatal to the man she loves."

Mr. Moto gathers the scrolls that have been scattered on the floor and starts to light a fire. Eleanor is untied by Tom who really believed that Eleanor and Koerger were romantically involved but with a smile, now believes everything is all right. Despite the pleadings of Eleanor Joyce and Tom Nelson, Moto then burns the scrolls to keep the promise he made to Prince Chung. "Now my friend can now face his ancestors without shame."

Commentary

Thank You, Mr. Moto probably ranks at the top of the *Mr. Moto* series owing from its plot which nicely mixes together mystery, intrigue, action, and romance. Norman Foster who is again the film's director and co-scenarist, keeps the film from being bogged down.

Again, Mr. Moto's disguise at the film's beginning is not enough to fool anyone watching the film. Wing, his Chinese servant, is perhaps the only one besides the police who doesn't recognize his master. Mr. Moto again shows that he can be a merciless killer when he stabs his attacker, three times in quick succession. As this occurs within the first several minutes of the film, one only wonders how many more will meet the same fate. To be fair however, Mr. Moto shows his sense of honor at the film's end when he dutifully burns all of the scrolls in fulfillment of a promise he made to the dead Prince Chung.

There are several voids in the film's plot plus some questions that remain unanswered from the series' first film, *Think Fast, Mr. Moto*. There is still the nagging point of who or what is Mr. Moto. Tom Nelson points Mr. Moto out to Eleanor Joyce and describes him as an adventurer, explorer, soldier of fortune, and one of the Orient's mysteries. Also, Tom claims that nobody knows very much about Mr. Moto except that when he shows up, something usually happens.

As for whom he works for, Mr. Moto tells Prince Chung that he was sent to Peiping to learn if the treasure of Genghis Khan exists and was to take the necessary steps to recover it, but he never reveals who his employer is. Furthermore, Moto tells Eleanor Joyce that he is a "confidential detective" for the International Association of Importers but only as a hobby, and it allows him to combine it with his profession of an importer. In the series' first entry, Mr. Moto introduces himself as the managing director of the Dai Nippon Trading Company. If this weren't enough, as he and Tom Nelson approach the city gate in a speeding car, Moto tells the guard, "I am Mr. Moto, International Police." Apparently Mr. Moto is a man of many trades.

The reason why Mr. Moto is invited to a garden party being held by a Colonel Tchernov is also not made clear. Moto even states that garden parties are seldom held in Peiping without a purpose and he questions what the host's purpose is. The viewer is shown that Moto can also be polite and cultured, being conversant in English, German, Chinese, and his native Japanese. He easily moves around in high-society and diplomatic settings when he is not murdering assailants.

The storyline formula is pretty much unchanged from the first film. Moto is apparently already on a case. He has a disguise. There's romance between a bachelor type and a pretty young woman. With a fast-moving plot, the film is also supported by a cast of capable actors including John Caradine, Philip Ahn, Pauline Frederick, and Sidney Blackmer.

Clockwise from the upper left: Philip Ahn, Pauline Frederick, Sig Rumann, and Sidney Blackmer.

The *Variety* review of January 12, 1938 errs a bit when the reviewer (Barn) incorrectly states, "Peter Lorre is ideal for the role of the sly Oriental who watches the smuggling outfits who try to steal his country's art treasures." Apparently the reviewer makes the connection that the story takes place in China. Yes, the valuable silk scroll treasures are Chinese, but Mr. Moto is *Japanese*. B. R. Crisler's review, printed in the *New York Times* on January 3, 1938, warns that "Nervous or squeamish souls may be disturbed by the continual thud of falling bodies." Mr. Moto is credited with three of the film's four murders.

Film Notes

Although this was the second film to be released in the *Mr. Moto* series, the film was not the second that went into production. Production of *Mr. Moto Takes a Chance* started in July 1937 but the film's release was held up, probably because of the Sino-Japanese War.[20] Instead, production then began on *Thank You, Mr. Moto*, adapted from the 1936 novel of the same title which was serialized in the *Saturday Evening Post* (February 8 to March 14, 1936). The film's production got underway in October 1937 and was completed two months later with the official release on December 24.

Like its preceding entry, changes were made in the characterizations compared with the novel. In the novel, Tom Nelson is a lawyer instead of being a diplomatic code clerk in the movie. In the novel, it is Nelson who is writing a book; in the film, it is Eleanor Joyce. Pu, the curio dealer of the novel now becomes Pieriera; Prince Tung is transformed into Prince Chung.

The plot had also undergone changes, possibly owing to the rising tensions in the Far East at that time. The novel in part, concerns itself with civil unrest in northern China and of several Japanese expansionists who desire military occupation—none of which is presented in the film. The

---

20   *Mr. Moto Takes a Chance* was released in June 1938 as the fourth film in the series.

novel also has Miss Joyce, representing an American museum, coming to China with $200,000 to acquire a set of eight Sung Dynasty paintings. These are owned by Prince Tung, which the prince agrees to sell. In the film, it is Moto competing against a group trying to acquire seven scroll paintings that show the location of the hidden tomb of Genghis Khan and its source of a vast treasure.[21] The prince has vowed that his family will never sell the five remaining scrolls in his possession.

The film is replete with the central theme of the vast treasure buried in the hidden tomb of Genghis Khan and subtle references to elements of Chinese history: the dowager empress,[22] and the Wei, T'ang, and Yu'an dynasties.[23] Furthermore, the film also refers to geographic locales in China, including the Gobi Desert,[24] Hun Ho River,[25] the Marco Polo

---

21 Genghis Khan (Mongolian for Universal Leader, c.1167-1227) was a Mongol leader and one of the great conquerors in the history of the world. He never learned to read and knew no language but Mongolian. However, he left behind a system of law, known as the Great Yasa, which was based upon Mongol customary law. Genghis Khan died in August 1227, at his summer quarters located in the district of Qingshui south of the Liupan Mountains in Gansu, China and according to legend, is buried in a secret location in Mongolia.

22 Tzu Hsi (1835-1908) was one of the concubines of the Ch'ing (Manchu) Emperor Hsien Feng, and she became the empress dowager when the emperor died in 1861 and his primary wife had no son. Tzu Hsi's five-year old son, Tung Chih, became emperor and she was named dowager empress.

23 The Wei Dynasty ruled China from 386 to 535. The T'ang Dynasty ruled China from 618 to 907. The Yu'an Dynasty was the period of Mongol rule over China from 1279 to 1368 initiated by the conquest of the Sung dynasty by Kublai Khan, a grandson of Genghis Khan. The Mongols, who had adopted the Chinese title Yu'an—meaning first—for their dynasty in 1271, defeated the last Sung emperor in 1279. The Yu'an Dynasty was succeeded by the Ming Dynasty in 1368.

24 The Gobi (Mongolian for place without water) Desert is Asia's largest desert, covering an area of about 500,000 square miles in Mongolia and the Inner Mongolia region of China and extends 1,000 miles east to west, with a maximum north to south measurement of 600 miles. It is a region of plateaus averaging 3,500 feet above sea level, broken by hills and by the Altai Mountains. The Gobi Desert became known through the writings of Marco Polo who reached it in the 13th century.

25 The Hun-ho (ho = river) in ancient times was known both as the Lugou and Sanggan River, although the local people call it either the Hun (small yellow) or the Heishui (black water) for its muddy water. During the Ch'ing Dynasty

Bridge,[26] and the city of Peiping, which has been known by many names throughout Chinese history.[27] The introduction of Japanese culture is also present with Moto playing the *samisen*[28] and Moto talks of *hara-kiri*[29] to Eleanor Joyce when he makes Colonel Tchernov's death look like a suicide.

---

when the river was dredged and its dykes strengthened to keep its riverbed from shifting, its name was changed to Yongding (eternal stability).

26   The well-known Lugou, or Marco Polo Bridge spans the Yongding River at Lugouqiao, about 10 miles southwest of Beijing (formerly Peiping/Peking). Construction started in June 1189 and was completed in March 1192. It is 866 feet long, 24 feet wide, has 11 arches, and 250 marble balustrades supporting 485 carved stone lions. First named the Guang Li Bridge, historical records show that the bridge was repaired six times in the Ming Dynasty (1368-1644) and seven times during the Ch'ing Dynasty (1644-1912).

The bridge is perhaps best known for the "Marco Polo Bridge Incident" when on July 7, 1937, Japanese troops illegally occupied a railway junction near Wanping and fighting erupted. This is considered by many to be the date that China entered WWII.

27   The city of Peiping (also Pei-p'ing) was previously called by other names such as Yanjing, Tat-Tu, and Shun-t'ien-fu, but from 1421 to 1911 during reign of the Mings and Manchus, the city was referred to as Peking—meaning northern capital. Following the establishment of the republic on February 12, 1912, the nationalist capital then rotated between Peking, Canton, and Hankow. In 1928 when Nanking was made the capital, Peking was changed to Peiping (northern peace). The Communist took control in 1949 and made Peiping its capital but restored the older name of Peking. In 1979 the Chinese government officially adopted the romanized spelling of its words using Pinyin, replacing the traditional Wade-Giles system used by English speakers. As a consequence, Peking officially became known as Beijing.

28   Popular secular music in Japan began in the 16th century with the introduction of the samisen from China. It resembles a banjo or lute, having a very long neck and three strings plucked with a plectrum.

29   Hara-kiri (literally, belly cutting) is the common Japanese language term for the practice of ritual suicide by self-disembowelment—sappuku is the formal term. It was the means to prove purity of one's own heart and soul, and was for many centuries of feudal Japan (1192-1868) the only honorable form of death for disgraced nobles and the samurai warrior class. The act is conducted as a very formal ceremony, requiring certain etiquette, witnesses and considerable preparation.

Under the bushido (way of the warrior) code of honor and conduct of the Japanese nobility, a Samurai was afraid of shame more than death itself, and he would rather die by his own hand before he would be humiliated or insulted. Obligatory until the Meiji Restoration (1868-1912), the ritual is still occasionally performed, but voluntarily.

For Pauline Frederick, who played the dowager Madame Chung, this was her last film in a career that included mainly silent films such as *Madame X* (1920)—perhaps her best known. She had asthma which limited her activities and almost nine months after the release of *Thank You, Mr. Moto*, she died from the disease on September 19, 1938 at the age of 55.

Thomas Beck appeared in his second *Mr. Moto* film but it would be one of his last films, having retired from acting in 1939 at age 30 when Twentieth Century-Fox reduced his salary for his political activities with the Screen Actors Guild. Although it cannot be verified from other sources, many viewers claim that Sen Yung (later Victor Sen Young) portrays the uncredited role of the elevator operator in Moto's hotel. In the following year, Young would portray Charlie Chan's Number Two son, Jimmy Chan, in 13 films with Sidney Toler (as Charlie Chan) at Fox and as Tommy Chan in five films with Roland Winters at Monogram.

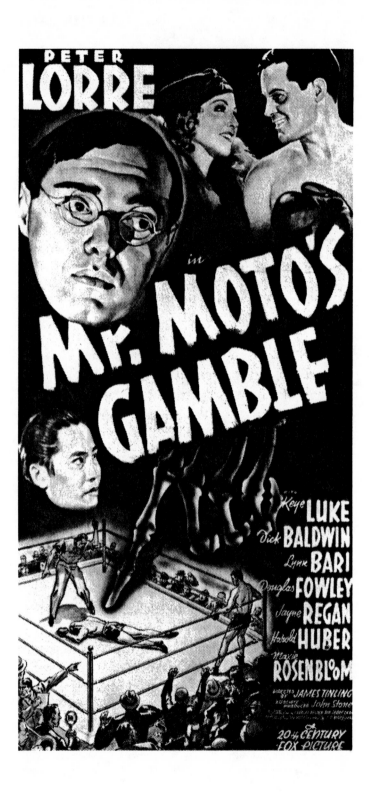

Mr. Moto's Gamble (1938)

Twentieth Century-Fox Film Corp. Distributed by Twentieth Century-Fox Film Corp. Released: March 25, 1938. Production: January 10 to mid-February 1938. Copyright Twentieth Century-Fox Film Corp., March 25, 1938; LP8170. Sound: Western Electric Mirrophonic Recording. B&W. 8 reels. 6,565 feet. 71 minutes. PCA certificate number 4053.

Producer: Sol M. Wurtzel.* Associate Producer: John Stone. Director: James Tinling. Dialogue Direction: Harvey G. Parry,* Arthur Berthelet,* and Lionel Bevans.* Assistant Director: Jasper Blystone* and Charles Faye.* Original Screen Play: Charles Belden and Jerry Cady. Photography: Lucien Andriot. Camera Operator: Edward Fitzgerald.* First Assistant Cameraman: Roger Sherman.* Second Assistant Cameraman: Edward Collins.* Gaffer: Jack McAvoy.* Art Direction: Bernard Herzbrun and Haldane Douglas. Film Editor: Nick DeMaggio. Assistant Cutter: Jack Lebowitz.* Costumes: Helen A. Myron. Wardrobe Girl: Gladys Isaacson.* Wardrobe Man: Jack Adams.* Musical Direction: Samuel Kaylin. Sound: Bernard A. Freericks and William H. Anderson. Assistant Sound: Joe Mazzoletti.* Boom Man: Harry Roberts.* Cableman: Fred Casey.* Make-up: Webster Phillips.* Production Manager: Ed. Ebele.* Unit Manager: Ben Wurtzel.* Script Clerk: Stanley Scheuer.* Grip: Hank Gersen.* Assistant Grip: Jimmie Reemer.* Props: Don Greenwood.* Assistant Props: Stanley Detlie* and Aaron Wolf.* Best Boy: Kenneth McDonald.* Still Photography: John Jenkins.*

Cast

Peter Lorre *as* . . . . Mr. Moto
Keye Luke . . . . Lee Chan
Dick Baldwin . . . . Bill Steele
Lynn Bari . . . . Penny Kendall
Douglas Fowley . . . . Nick Crowder
Jayne Regan . . . . Linda Benton
Harold Huber . . . . Lieutenant Riggs
Maxie Rosenbloom . . . . [Horace "Knockout"] Wellington
John Hamilton . . . . Philip Benton
George E. Stone . . . . [Jerry] Connors
Bernard Nedell . . . . Clipper McCoy
Charles Williams . . . . Gabby Marden
Ward Bond . . . . Biff Moran
Cliff Clark . . . . [Tom "Mac"] McGuire
Edward Marr . . . . Sammy
Lon Chaney, Jr. . . . . Joey
Russ Clark . . . . Frankie Stanton
Pierre Watkin . . . . District Attorney [Joe]
Charles D. Brown . . . . Editor [Scotty]
Paul Fix* . . . . Gangster
Dick Dickinson* . . . . Knock-down timer
Fred Kelsey* . . . . Mahoney
Ralph Dunn,* David Newell,* Frank McGlynn, Jr.* . . . . . . Detectives
George Magrill,* Bob Ryan,* Eddie Hart,* James Blaine,*
     Harry Strang,* Stanley Blystone,* Lee Shumway,*
     Dick Rush,* Adrian Morris,* Max Wagner* . . . . Policemen
Jack Stoney* . . . . Kid Grant
Edwin Stanley,* Landers Stevens* . . . . Doctors
Frank Fanning* . . . . Turnkey
Allen Mathews* . . . . Handler
Lester Dorr,* Allen Fox,* Franklin Parker,* Dick French* . . . Reporters
Emmett Vogan* . . . . Fingerprint man
Edward Earle* . . . . Medical examiner
Gladden James* . . . . Cashier
Sherry Hall* . . . . Ticket taker
Matty Roubert* . . . . Elevator boy

William E. Coe* . . . . Timekeeper
Bob Perry,* George Blake,* Larry McGrath* . . . . Referees
Gary Breckner* . . . . Announcer
Dan Toby* . . . . Fight announcer
Joe Gray,* Tommy Herman,* Pete De Grasse* . . . . Fighters
Stanley Mack,* Jack Gargan* . . . . Ushers
Syd Saylor* . . . . Hotel clerk
Don Brodie* . . . . Ticket seller
Arthur Gardner* . . . . Elevator boy
Irving Bacon* . . . . Sheriff [Tuttle]
Olin Howland* . . . . Deputy sheriff
Matty Fain,* Harrison Greene,* Wilbur Mack,* Dick Elliott* . . . . Gamblers
George Chandler* . . . . Man in fight crowd
Gloria Roy* . . . . unamed
Chester Clute* . . . . Boxing detective

*Unbilled

"In poker, the man with the poorer cards very often wins on a bluff."
—Mr. Moto to Lt. Riggs

The Story

Mr. Moto is just about finishing up the day's class in a college criminology course he is teaching. After giving an assignment for the next
meeting, he reminds the class that if they find the problem difficult, "There
is no situation that science *and* skill can't master." One of the students
however is a police detective and challenges Moto's statement. Moto
accepts the challenge and confidently dares the detective to pull a gun on
him to demonstrate his point. When the cop starts to reach for his gun,
Mr. Moto quickly uses his ju-jitsu skills to disarm the cop by throwing him
to the floor.

Lee Chan (Keye Luke), Charlie Chan's Number One son also happens
to be taking the course and now notices that his watch has been stolen.
Moto questions "Knockout" Wellington (Maxie Rosenbloom), another

student who is an ex-boxer and has been sitting next to Lee all evening.

"What time is it Mr. Wellington?"

Wellington pulls out Lee's watch as if were his own. When confronted with the purloined timepiece as evidence, Wellington confesses that he is the culprit and discloses that he is a kleptomaniac—he cannot help taking things that attract his eye. To make matters worse, Wellington doesn't remember from where or whom he takes the objects but Mr. Moto carefully warns the former boxer that he must change his ways or his first case as a detective will be the arrest of himself. Wellington tells the Japanese teacher that this is precisely why he is taking the course—to help him remember. Moto then commends his effort saying, "To recognize one's faults requires intelligence; to admit them requires courage."

Once class is dismissed, Lee approaches Mr. Moto and tells him that his father, Charlie Chan, sends his regards. However, Lee confesses that, against the wishes of his detective father, he'd rather be a detective instead of studying art at the university. Mr. Moto confides in Lee that his parents wanted him to be an acrobat and assures him that he will write his famous father that Lee is his most promising student.

Lt. Riggs (Harold Huber), head of New York's homicide squad, stops by the class to pick up Moto to join him at a boxing match that evening between Bill Steele (Dick Baldwin) and Frankie Stanton (Russ Clark). Mr. Moto invites Lee to accompany him and Riggs mentions to Lee, "I know your old man well. He's got plenty on the ball, eh Moto?"

Mr. Moto politely replies, "Oh, we are but floundering amateurs by contrast."

At the arena before the fight, gambler Nick Crowder (Douglas Fowley) bets $10,000 with bookie Clipper McCoy (Bernard Nedell) at 3-to-1 odds "on a hunch" that Stanton will not come out for the fifth round. Cautious, McCoy warns Crowder that Stanton's manager Jerry Connors (George E. Stone) better not help throw the fight. Crowder quips that McCoy would suspect his own grandmother and the bookie replies, "Yeh, but *you're not* my grandmother."

"Wanna bet?" goads the gambler.

Lt. Riggs, Moto, and Lee sit at ringside alongside Philip Benton (John

An enthusiastic Keye Luke joins Harold Huber and a calm Peter Lorre at ringside.

Hamilton) and his snooty daughter Linda (Jayne Regan) who is interested in Bill Steele even though he likes sports reporter Penny Kendall (Lynn Bari). The winner of the match will then fight world champion Biff Moran (Ward Bond) eight weeks later. Lt. Riggs makes a friendly $10 wager with Benton that Stanton will beat Steele. Riggs lets Mr. Moto know that Benton is president of the company that owns the arena but never bets more than a few dollars and his daughter Linda "has her nose so high in the air that she'll drown in a rainstorm!"

Prior to the start of the fight, Frankie Stanton already has a cut over his left eye and Steele's manager, "Mac" McGuire (Cliff Clark) encourages his boxer to "work on that eye." When the bell rings, nothing much happens until the second round when Steele is knocked down but recovers sufficiently to finish the round. In between rounds, McCoy stops by Steele's corner and asks if Steele could finish off Stanton. Steele confidently tells the bookie that "I'm shooting the works. It's this round or never." In the

other corner, the fight referee tells Connors that cut over Stanton's eye is bad and he might have to stop the fight. Connors then applies collodion to stop the bleeding.[30]

In the third round Bill Steele unleashes a flurry of punches that finally knocks out Stanton and Steele is declared the winner. Crowder sees McCoy in the arena's lobby and reminds the bookie that he'll stop by later to collect on his hunch. Also in the lobby are Lt. Riggs, Mr. Moto, Lee, and Knockout, who gives an animated blow-by-blow replay of the fight. However Moto observes that Wellington is wearing a finely tailored overcoat—one which he didn't have on earlier at the arena. Frustrated, Wellington concludes that he must have taken it and Moto suggests that the criminology student search for clues as to its real owner.

---

30   Collodion is a highly flammable, colorless or yellowish syrupy solution of pyroxylin, ether, and alcohol. It is used as an adhesive to close small wounds and hold surgical dressings in topical medications, and is used for making photographic plates.

Lt. Riggs is then summoned to Stanton's dressing room and is told by the ring doctor (Edwin Stanley) that Stanton is now dead. The doctor says there is evidence of strangulation which usually follows a concussion, such as when Stanton hit his head when he fell. Mr. Moto however presses the doctor further when he notices a discoloration around the injured eye which has increased after death—a clue the doctor previously ignored. Moto then speculates that a "foreign element" came in contact with the cut, and press agent Gabby Marden (Charles Williams), who works for Benton, asks if it was poison.

Mr. Moto retrieves a dried bit of collodion from Stanton's brow and McGraw angrily remarks that Connors had applied collodion to Stanton's cut during the fight. Connors however tries to cast aside any inference that he would kill his own fighter and throw away any chance at a title fight. In a heated exchange that follows, McGraw then insinuates that Steele used to be Connor's fighter but was gotten rid of when Steele refused to throw a fight. Connors refutes this and says he simply kicked him out.

Observing this action nearby, Lt. Riggs then tells both Connors and McGraw to stop their shouting match but Mr. Moto, having seen what interesting information the squabble has produced, reminds Riggs that "Much information can obtained from tongues loosened by anger." However, the chance has now gone and the two managers are no longer volunteering any information.

Lt. Riggs then presses Connors as to the location of the bottle of collodion he used earlier for Stanton's cut. Worried immediately after Stanton's death, Connors threw the original bottle out a dressing room window and gives the policeman a different bottle to examine. Moto successfully convinces both Riggs and the fight doctor that the only way to be certain how Stanton died is to have an autopsy.

Later that evening, Philip Benton who earlier bragged to Lt. Riggs that he never bets more than a few dollars, quietly calls Clipper McCoy to say that he will send over a check for $10,000 the next day to cover his losing bet on the fight. A few moments later Nick Crowder and his henchman Joey (Lon Chaney, Jr.) enter McCoy's office to collect on the winning bet. The bookie reveals he had no time to lay off the bet and is now on the hook for the entire $30,000 owed to Crowder. This payment is not what is troubling McCoy though. As a member of a gambling syndicate, McCoy is obligated to pay 20 percent on all the syndicate's out-of-town losses. Apparently one or more individuals made the same incredible bet that Crowder did in six different cities—bets that total an additional $100,000—and McCoy is not yet sure if Crowder has anything to do with the other losses.

The autopsy concludes that Frankie Stanton was murdered with a drug called amarone and the poison was also found on Steele's glove. Lt. Riggs' further questioning of suspects McGraw, Connors, McCoy, Crowder, and Steele yields no new facts. However Steele is subsequently indicated by a grand jury, charged with manslaughter, jailed, and suspended by the boxing commission. Steele's girlfriend Penny Kendall then convinces Scotty (Charles D. Brown), her editor at *The Daily Chronicle*, that their newspaper should put up the $25,000 bond. She will then write an emotional human interest story to gain public support which should help sell papers. When Penny arrives at the jail with check in hand to post the bond, she finds Bill Steele about to leave jail with Linda Benton who has already paid the bond with a check from her father. Linda mentions aloud that it was *her* idea—designed to further anger Penny. After Linda and Bill leave, Penny

Mr. Moto's Gamble was originally intended as a *Charlie Chan* picture with Warner Oland (left) and Keye Luke as his Number One Son, Lee.

then tears up the newspaper's certified check.

In Mr. Moto's next criminology class, Moto shows the class a police photo of one of the boxing gloves used in the fatal fight, drawing the class's attention to the stain left by the poison on the glove. Knockout Wellington draws a big laugh from the class when he tells Lee Chan that he has already figured out who did it and closed the case—"Nobody. I couldn't get no clues, so I called it suicide."

Passing the photo around and listening to the dubious conclusions of the class members, Moto respectfully reminds his students that the basis of all deductions is that of careful observation. He then systematically demonstrates many possibilities of how the poison could have been applied to the glove. The only one that fits the pattern on the glove is that the poison was applied from outside the ring—as if it was somehow squirted on the glove. A simple in-class experiment with the aid of a class member confirms his deduction. Wellington elicits another laugh after he reluctantly admits that he now has to open the case again.

Outside the classroom, Lee Chan tells Wellington that he is still baffled how the murderer could squirt the poison without being seen. Wellington suggests the murderer had a hose but admits it would have been seen by the spectators. The ex-boxer leaves the building and starts to put on his overcoat but it is too short and tight. He concludes that someone stole "his" coat. In reality, the coat is Mr. Moto's, which Wellington has mistakenly exchanged with the finely tailored one he took at the Steele-Stanton boxing match.

Wellington tells Lee Chan that he now has to get to Steele's training camp because McGraw has hired him as a rubdown man. Conveniently, there is a sporty convertible parked in front of them. Lee remarks that the engine is running but Knockout gives the reason he leaves the engine running is because he can never remember where he puts the keys. Wellington and Lee get in and they drive off, except it is not Wellington's car. As is often the case, Lee is the gullible follower.

When Mr. Moto goes to the cloak room to put on his coat, it is too big and he realizes a switch has been made. To his good luck however, Moto notices a label from a Detroit tailor on the coat's inside pocket that identifies the coat's owner as John Howard—a name Mr. Moto does not recognize. Better still, Moto also observes a stain just below the label that matches the poison stain found on Steele's glove. Subsequent chemical analysis in the police laboratory identifies the stain as coming from amarone—the same poison that killed Stanton. With this evidence, Lt. Riggs is now determined to find John Howard.

At Biff Moran's training camp, Philip Benton and Gabby Marden are talking to Nick Crowder about the fight to get ideas for a promotional campaign. Clipper McCoy also shows up so that he can set up the betting odds. When confronted by Crowder and his fighter, McCoy tells both that he will give 3-to-1 odds that Steele knocks out Moran inside of eight rounds—a wager Crowder quickly accepts.

The bookie remarks about the nice training camp Crowder has and that it must cost lots of money for its upkeep. The gambler then brags, "It comes easy." Still smarting from the financial losses from the last fight however, McCoy then accuses Crowder of getting hunches at $100,000 a hunch but Nick is confused, reminding Clipper that he won only $30,000. McCoy accuses Crowder of getting someone to place the same unusual bet in six other cities and he also got hooked for 20 percent of those losses.

As Benton and Gabby they are about to leave, Nick Crowder orders Joey to tail the pair. Unaware they are being followed, Benton asks Gabby Marden if he overheard the argument between Crowder and McCoy—information that Crowder laid off $100,000 in bets around the country so as not to knock the odds down at the fight. Despite what they heard, Benton wonders if it can be proved. Gabby volunteers to find out and take the next plane. Benton tells him to spend whatever it costs.

In his office, Lt. Riggs finally receives a physical description of the mysterious John Howard from the Detroit tailor who made the overcoat, but it proves virtually worthless—"Medium height. Medium build. Medium complexion. I'd have to be a medium to find Howard from the description like that Detroit tailor gives me!" says the frustrated cop who vows to find Howard even if he has to turn the town upside down.

Gabby then calls Riggs from Steele's training camp, letting him know that someone took a shot at him. Riggs tells Moto and Penny Kendall that

Gabby didn't see who shot at him—"Perhaps it was another mystery man like John Howard" surmises Riggs.

"Maybe it was John Howard," adds Mr. Moto with a smile.

After Riggs, Moto, and Penny arrive at the training camp, Riggs gets no further questioning the suspects but Moto offers, "I have often noticed that the dog and the human are very much alike. Each will go to any length to obtain something he desires, or to destroy something he believes dangerous."

Moto then resolves that someone considered Gabby dangerous because he must know something about the Stanton murder. Benton then confesses he and Gabby decided to make a quiet investigation after they overheard Nick and Clipper arguing about the betting losses. Adding to the revelations, McCoy tells Lt. Riggs that Benton also had a $10,000 losing bet on the fight.

In the meantime, the owner of the car that Wellington took has called the police. On a country road, Wellington and Lee are stopped and are arrested by Sheriff Tuttle (Irving Bacon) for speeding. Wellington is also driving a stolen car without a license. Tuttle contacts Lt. Riggs and brings the pair to the training camp. Mr. Moto congratulates Tuttle for capturing two "extremely desperate criminals" and suggests that the sheriff keep them in safe custody until called for. Lee protests, but Moto tells Riggs with a straight face, "The usual way to avoid trouble is to lock it out. In this case, we lock it in."

Acting on a tip where John Howard is staying, Riggs and Moto are told John Howard is now in the county morgue and that he died from heart failure. However, Moto feels Howard's death, like the others connected with this case, is too convenient and suggests Lt. Riggs order an autopsy and check the fingerprints of the dead man. A short time later, Lt. Riggs is told that from the fingerprints, the dead man is Whitey Goodman, an ex-con out on parole. Riggs is also told that the heart failure was due to amarone.

In the office of the District Attorney (Pierre Watkin), Lt. Riggs then concludes that Goodman, posing as John Howard, was simply a fall guy, having made the bets for someone else, and was killed by the person he was working for after he collected the money. However, the D.A. is still not convinced that Steele isn't the person Goodman was working for and won't lift the indictment against Steele. However, Riggs only wants the D.A. to have the boxing commission lift Steele's suspension to permit the championship fight go on that evening as scheduled while Mr. Moto hopes to expose the identity of the murder. The D.A. exclaims, "If I were sure of that, I'd sell tickets myself."

Moto philosophically adds, "To reveal a snake, one must overturn a rock." Convinced the plan could work, the D.A. then places a call to the boxing commissioner.

Following the weigh-in at the arena, Nick Crowder wants to know from Mr. Moto who pulled strings to get the fight on tonight. Moto replies, "Some people save strings. I pull them" and defends his interest in seeing the fight go on because of his promise to the D.A. to unmask Stanton's murderer. However Clipper McCoy appears bored of the process, wanting Moto to get it over with now instead of later. Inside the vacant arena, the viewer sees a mysterious figure placing a gun attached to a clock under the ring mat and aims it at the seat Mr. Moto will be sitting during the fight. The clock is carefully set for 10 o'clock.

While Lee Chan and Knockout Wellington are being held in jail by Sheriff Tuttle, the two plan how to get released. Suddenly, Wellington pulls out a gun from his overcoat pocket. Lee cautions that the gun might go off, but Knockout shows that it is a toy water gun by squirting its contents onto a cell wall containing a paper calendar. Moments later they see the paper smoking, as if were attacked by some kind of acid. Lee exclaims that it is the gun involved with Frankie Stanton's murder. The two finally escape from jail by tricking the not-too bright sheriff and they head off to the arena with the murder gun.

Before the fight Penny kisses Bill Steele, wishes him well, and then castigates Linda for only caring for a winner and having dumped other fighters once they lost a fight. With the hidden gun pointed at him, Mr. Moto now carefully watches his suspects as the fight begins.

In the first round, Moran gets the best of Steele and knocks him down twice. When it looks like he will be counted out, Steele is saved by the bell.

Between rounds, Linda Benton, sitting with her father near the ringside, is told by an usher that Mac McGraw wants her to come down to Steele's corner where she gives Steele some vocal encouragement. However McGraw is annoyed by her presence and orders her to get back to her seat. Surprised, Linda tells McGraw that she thought he had sent for her, but the trainer knows nothing of this. As she starts to return to her seat, she passes Mr. Moto who poltely offers her the vacant seat next to him.

The action of the second round finds Steele firmly in control. Unlike the frenzy exhibited by those in the audience, Moto is cautiously quiet, carefully watching everything, and is apparently still unaware that the hidden gun pointed at him is soon set to go off. Steele finally opens a barrage of punches and knocks out the champion.

Philip Benton comes over to Moto's seat and suggests that they all go back to Steele's dressing room to offer their congratulations. However Mr. Moto reminds Benton and Lt. Riggs that he hopes to catch the murderer within a few minutes and insists that Linda remain in the seat next to him. Benton protests that if the killer is around, his daughter will be safer in his upstairs office. Frustrated that he can't change Moto's mind and with the seconds ticking by, Benton panics and reaches under the ring mat and disarms the hidden gun.

"Thank you, Mr. Benton" says Mr. Moto with both Linda and Penny staring in disbelief. "Your own actions have proved that you are the murderer."

Benton then charges Moto had almost committed murder by trying prove it, but Moto confesses that he earlier had took the precaution of looking in the arena, finding the gun and clock assembly, and had removed the bullets. Moto tells that he had a hunch that the murderer would try to stop him after he had announced he would catch the murderer that evening during the championship fight.

Having been exposed, Philip Benton frantically pushes his way past Riggs and heads to the lobby where he takes the elevator to his office. When Benton exits the elevator to his office, Clipper McCoy there is waiting for him with a gun. He found out that Benton reneged on a Chicago bet for $50,000. Benton pleads that he made that bet good and

McCoy interrupts, "Sure, with the dough you gypped me out of from the Stanton fight." Benton then reminds McCoy that he had bet on Stanton with McCoy and lost $10,000, a claim McCoy dismisses as a cover up. In desperation, Benton tries to flee but is shot and killed by McCoy who then calmly takes the elevator down to the lobby.

Meanwhile, Lt. Riggs and Mr. Moto climb the stairs and enter Benton's office to find the dead body. Riggs feared that Benton would kill himself but Moto counters that Benton was shot in the back and no gun is seen. Moto then calmly suggests that they wait in the office for Benton's killer to return by the only way he could have left—the elevator. A few moments later the elevator door opens and McCoy is seen in custody between two policemen.

Lee and Knockout finally arrive at the arena and when Wellington is about to remember where he found the water gun that will convict the murderer, Mr. Moto informs Lee and Knockout that the murderer has already been caught, convicted, and executed—pointing to the body inside Benton's office.

Back in his classroom once again, Mr. Moto explains the series of events leading to why he suspected Benton. He also thanks two of the members of the class, Lee and Knockout, for their help. Moto announces that the term has ended and he needs to catch a plane. Reaching into his vest pocket for his pocket watch, Moto finds it missing from the chain and looks straight at Wellington with a smile. Wellington returns the watch and thanks Mr. Moto for helping him now remember from where he takes things. To test Wellington's newly acquired ability, Moto asks from whom Wellington stole the wallet Moto pulls from the ex-boxer's coat pocket. Knockout claims it is his but Moto corrects him—it belongs to Lee Chan. "Class dismissed."

Commentary

The third *Mr. Moto* entry introduces a number of "firsts." After two films, Mr. Moto is actually a detective this time as he teaches a college criminology class for sleuthing wannabees. Also, this is the first film to use comic relief along with the requisite romantic couple, the first (and only) match up between Mr. Moto and one of Charlie Chan's 14 offspring—Number One son Lee Chan, and the first film in which Mr. Moto doesn't kill anyone. If, with the exception of Peter Lorre's name, looking at the cast and crew lists makes you think that this is a Charlie Chan picture instead of Mr. Moto, you are right. Both series are produced by Twentieth Century-Fox and the film originally started out as *Charlie Chan at the Ringside* but was soon reworked as *Mr. Moto's Gamble*.

The film opens in a scene reminiscent of that in *Charlie Chan at the Race Track* (1935) where Charlie Chan is demonstrating the use of the observation of clues and deductive reasoning to arrive to the correct conclusion. Mr. Moto later uses another technique similar to that employed in the same *Charlie Chan* film (using blood stains), to deduce how the stain was left by the poison on the glove used to kill Frankie Stanton. The *Hollywood Reporter* review of March 12, 1938 praises the film saying, "A combination of whodunit, adventure and prize fight yarn, it moves as a fast pace through engaging counterpoint construction."

Although this film was hurriedly changed to a *Mr. Moto* production, there *is* continuity in the storyline that actually makes sense. First, Lee explains to Mr. Moto that he is in New York as an art student. Charlie Chan aficionados will easily recall that in the last film before Warner Oland died, *Charlie Chan at Monte Carlo* (1937), Lee explains to the Monte Carlo police chief (played by Harold Huber) that although he prefers detective work, in the opinion of his father he is an artist and is on his way to Paris to exhibit some of his paintings. In *Charlie Chan in Honolulu*, which was produced about nine months after *Mr. Moto's Gamble*, Number Two son Jimmy, in explaining Keye Luke's absence from the series, remarks to his father that the older brother Lee now attends art school in New York.

However, there are two things that are not explained. One is the reason for Mr. Moto teaching a criminology class. Of course this could have been part of the original *Charlie Chan* plot. Then there is no explanation for Lee Chan being a student in Mr. Moto's class when he could learn from the master—his father. After all, Mr. Moto reminds Lt. Riggs, "Oh, we are but floundering amateurs by contrast."

The comic relief provided by both Maxie Rosenbloom and Keye Luke is somewhat overdone but it does give Lorre a chance to show his lighter side. In its review of April 13, 1938, *Variety* is pleased with "the quality of Rosenbloom's buffonery [sic]." Nonetheless, the film would have been better with only one person to play off the funny parts, as is often done with Chan's children in the earlier *Chan* films. Since a significant portion of the film was already shot before reworking it as a *Mr. Moto* entry, some compromises had to be made and the humor could have been a holdover from the initial *Charlie Chan* project with very little room to maneuver. Unfortunately, the use of humor will now serve as a requisite feature for virtually all the remaining films in the *Mr. Moto* series with Peter Lorre.

Film Notes

Mr. Moto's Gamble, whose working titles were *Mr. Moto at Ringside* and *Mr. Moto's Diary*, was originally planned as a *Charlie Chan* film with Warner Oland. Originally titled, *Charlie Chan at the Ringside* with working titles of *Charlie Chan at the Arena* and *Charlie Chan at the Fights*, Twentieth Century-Fox started production on January 10, 1938. While filming, Warner Oland and the studio had a disagreement and Oland left the set one day and did not return. Seven days after production began, Darryl Zanuck scrapped the picture, having finally been fed up with Warner Oland's drinking and absences from the set, and put Oland on suspension. From studio records, $93,820.59 was spent on production up to this point.

On January 24, 1938, Twentieth Century-Fox decided to salvage parts of *Charlie Chan at the Ringside* and began the production of reworking it into *Mr. Moto's Gamble*. Correspondence from producer Sol M. Wurtzel revealed that $46,341.10 was saved by converting the original project to the *Mr. Moto* series and he suggested that the amount of $39,979.49 be billed to Warner Oland. It is not known if this was actually done as Oland, eager to see his homeland once more, sailed to his native Sweden where he died of bronchial pneumonia on August 6, 1938 at age 58.

In this new movie, Lee Chan, long known as Charlie Chan's Number One son, is now as an assistant to the Japanese detective Mr. Moto played by Peter Lorre. All but two of the original *Ringside* cast were used in the new

Clockwise from the upper left: Lynn Bari, Douglas Fowley, John Hamilton, and "Slapsie Maxie" Rosenbloom.

film. Warner Oland and his *Charlie Chan* character was replaced by Peter Lorre as Mr. Moto, and Paul Hurst was replaced by Harold Huber as Lt. Riggs. The film was released on March 25, 1938.

Keye Luke is perhaps best known in his film career as portraying Charlie Chan's Number One son Lee Chan in ten films. With Warner Oland's death in 1938, Luke's character was replaced by Sen Yung in the role of Jimmy Chan. Prior to his acting career, Luke was a talented artist and entered the film industry as a billboard designer and caricaturist.

Maxie Rosenbloom, who played "Knockout" Wellington and provided half of the film's comic relief, was once the World Light Heavyweight champion from 1930 to 1934. As a right-handed fighter, he often appeared to strike his opponents with open gloves and thus picked up the nickname "Slapsie Maxie." His 16-year pro career record included 210 wins (19 KO's), 38 losses, and 26 draws. He appeared in nearly 60 movies, often as a punch-drunk fighter.

As for other actors, Lon Chaney, Jr. plays a small part as Nick Crowder's henchman Joey. Chaney would go on to be best known for his portrayal of the wolf man and other villains in Universal's horror films. John Hamilton, who played the murderer Philip Benton would be perhaps best known two decades later as Perry White, the editor of the *Daily Planet* in the television episodes of *The Adventures of Superman* from 1952 to 1957 and a number of movies made from the *Superman* series. Ward Bond, the burley actor who portrayed the boxer Biff Moran would later appear in a second *Mr. Moto* film, *Mr. Moto in Danger Island* (1939). In the mid-'50s, he gained his greatest fame as the star of TV's "Wagon Train."

Mr. Moto Takes a Chance (1938)

Twentieth Century-Fox Film Corp. Distributed by Twentieth Century-Fox Film Corp. Released: June 24, 1938. New York opening: June 11, 1938. Production: July 19 to mid-Aug 1937. Copyright Twentieth Century-Fox Film Corp., June 24, 1938; LP 8380. Sound: Western Electric Mirrophonic Recording. B&W. 7 reels. 5,736 feet. 57 or 63 minutes. PCA certificate number 3642.

Executive producer: Sol M. Wurtzel. Director: Norman Foster. Screen play: Lou Breslow and John Patrick. Original story: Willis Cooper and Norman Foster, based on the character "Mr. Moto" created by J. P. Marquand. Photography: Virgil Miller, A.S.C. Art direction: Albert Hogsett. Film editor: Nick DeMaggio. Costumes: Herschel. Sound: Bernard Freericks and Harry M. Leonard. Musical direction: Samuel Kaylin. Assistant directors: William Eckhardt* and Tom Dudley.* Camera operator: Irving Rosenberg.* Assistant cameramen: Charles Bohny and Ed Garvin.* Gaffer: Fred Hall.* Wardrobe man: Ernest Rotchy.* Wardrobe girl: Viola Richards.* Assistant sound: L. B. Dix.* Boom man: Paul Gilbert.* Cableman: P. Kelly.* Hair stylist: Marie Livingston.* Makeup: Bill Cooley.* Production manager: Edward Ebele.* Script clerk: Jack Vernon.* Grip: Roger Murphy.* Props: Joe Behm.* Assistant prop men: Ancil Whitlow* and Elmer Poggi.* Best boy: John Grady* and Frank Gilroy.* Still photographer: Steve McNulty.* Stand-ins: Emily Baldwin,* Rollo Dix,* and Delmar Costello.*

Cast

Peter Lorre *as* . . . . Mr. Moto
Rochelle Hudson . . . . Victoria Mason
Robert Kent . . . . Marty Weston
J. Edward Bromberg . . . . Rajah Ali
Chick Chandler . . . . Chick Davis
George Regas . . . . Bokor
Frederick Vogeding . . . . [Capt.] Zimmerman
Gloria Roy* . . . . Keema
Al Kikume* . . . . Yao
James B. Leong* . . . . native

*Unbilled

"I'm sorry, but I find it wise never to interfere with the customs of
other people."

—Mr. Moto to Victoria Mason

The Story

Victoria Mason (Rochelle Hudson) is attempting to fly around the
world alone. At one stage of her journey, she radios the authorities at Ran-
goon, Burma that she is currently passing over the ruins of Angkor. She
then looks at a map and makes it appear her next destination will be the
small village kingdom of Tong Moi in the neighboring country above
Siam—Laos above present-day Thailand.

Meanwhile in the jungle near Tong Moi, Mr. Moto is dressed impec-
cably with a pith helmet, white suit, white shoes, white gloves, and is
leading an archaeological dig among the area's ancient ruins. Also in the
area are American cameramen Marty Weston (Robert Kent) and Chick
Davis (Chick Chandler) shooting film for future newsreel stories. When

her plane approaches Tong Moi, Vicki activates a flare and tosses it into the rear of the plane, making it appear the plane is on fire. Both Moto and the cameramen notice the smoke from the plane and its subsequent crash in the jungle.

Moto sees that Miss Mason was able to parachute to safety and he rushes to help the aviatrix with her parachute. After she tells him about her attempt to fly around the world and Mr. Moto apologizes for his ignorance confessing, "You will excuse me but we are so out touch with events here in Tong Moi." In return, Moto explains that he has been busy excavating the ruins there.

he crash of Vicki's plane has not gone unnoticed by Bokor (George Regas), the influential high priest of Tong Moi who now arrives on the scene. Moto introduces Vicki to Bokor and convinces him to take her to Tong Moi where its ruler, Rajah Ali (J. Edward Bromberg), will be pleased to meet her. Before departing though, Vicki cautions Mr. Moto not to let his men get too near the plane wreck, fearing the gas tanks might explode. However Moto feels whatever danger there might be has already passed—a suspicion confirmed when he finds a used flare, the real cause of the smoke, among the plane's wreckage. Moto leaves for the ancient ruins and then sends a note written in Japanese via a carrier pigeon about Vicki's arrival with details to follow later. However it is not clear who is the recipient of Moto's message.

When she arrives with Bokor at the village, Vicki is introduced to Rajah Ali who is very pleased that she escaped from the crash unhurt and wants to extend his hospitality to her. Despite the objections of Bokor, Ali insists that she stay as his guest for several weeks. Marty and Chick suddenly arrive and immediately start setting up to shoot some film without permission for the newsreel back home. Ali is angry and demands to know who they are and what they are doing. Chick answers, "Don't get sore, your Honor. It's a big scoop for us," but Ali doesn't understand American slang. Nonetheless, Marty commands, "Keep your pants on King. We get the picture!" Their pushy and somewhat impolite behavior to the rajah causes Bokor to remind the two cameramen, "You are addressing His Highness, the Rajah of Tong Moi!"

Eventually, the ruler is flattered that he will be on film welcoming the attractive Miss Mason to Tong Moi but Bokor wants the cameramen to leave with their camera—it is sorcery and is not permitted. Chick retorts, "Aw general, no devil in box. It's just a movie camera." Marty wants the rajah to tell "Dracula" (Bokor) that they are not going to hurt anybody. Nonetheless, Bokor is adamant that the gods will not be pleased if the camera captures the ruler's image.

Marty then has the bright idea of having one of the native women appear in the picture with Vicki and the rajah. "Here honey, you get in the picture too. Step right up there," as Chick coaxes one woman but Bokor tells him that she is the rajah's favorite wife, Keema (Gloria Roy). Fortunately, Rajah Ali is more enlightened and less superstitious than Bokor and declares that the cinema is not dangerous.

Moments after the filming starts, Keema suddenly falls dead from no apparent cause. Bokor seizes the moment, accusing the white devils—Marty and Chick—for causing Keema's death with their camera and he orders the

A publicity still with Robert Kent, Rochelle Hudson, Peter Lorre, and J. Edward Bromberg.

A publicity still with Robert Kent, Rochelle Hudson, Peter Lorre, and J. Edward Bromberg.

cameramen taken prisoner with a trial before the gods. Mr. Moto suddenly arrives on the scene and after hearing the explanation of events from Vicki, Bokor adds that he had warned them, but to no avail. Vicki wants Mr. Moto to tell Rajah Ali and Bokor it is not possible for a camera to kill, but Moto declares, "Everything is possible, here in the Orient."

After Marty and Chick are taken away, Vicki pleads for the rajah to stop Bokor, but he tells her that his power, which is granted by the French, is limited and there is very little he can do. He further explains he is allowed to keep his small kingdom only as long there is peace, and if he doesn't favor Bokor, the high priest will create conflict among his subjects. Nonetheless, the rajah assures Vicki he will talk to Bokor the next day on the Americans' behalf.

Marty and Chick are taken by Bokor to a hidden temple in the jungle for their trial before the gods. As a test, Yao (Al Kikume), one of Bokor's followers, touches Marty's arm with a white-hot rod which burns his skin signifying they are guilty. Bokor then appeals to the gods to show them a sign if they would be offended if Marty and Chick are killed. As expected, nothing happens and Bokor orders his men to throw the two cameramen down a deep well as their punishment.

Suddenly a fire erupts in front of one of the temple's stone images and halts the executions. An old guru then emerges from the temple and orders the Americans be removed from the sacred temple grounds. But Bokor claims to be the high priest of Shiva and is furious at the guru who dares to give orders to him. In response, the guru reminds Bokor that the fiery *Naga* is a sign that the gods are angry and accuses Bokor of being a fraud.

The guru tells Bokor that he is on a long pilgrimage from the Himalayas and has powers allowing him to see through walls and the dishonesty of men. Bokor challenges the guru's claims, requesting the guru show some act of sorcery for him to see. The guru responds, "We of the higher knowledge disdain the tricks of conjurers."

But Bokor presses further, "Perhaps you do not know the ancient

Director Norman Foster oversees the shooting of a jungle scene on the studio's back lot with cinematographer Virgil Miller behind the camera.

secrets," and commands Yao to fetch a round basket which is placed in front of the guru, revealing a cobra when the lid is removed. The guru proceeds to control the snake, directing it towards Bokor who now is afraid of it and pleads for the guru to stop. "Snake charming is an inferior art. In my country, it is done to amuse the feebleminded," admonishes the guru who in turn challenges Bokor to do the same to him but Bokor refuses, claiming the guru is a demon.

The next morning Mr. Moto is walking in the jungle and crosses paths with Vicki, Marty, and Chick. He remarks that he has heard of the two cameramen's close brush with death the previous night and is glad they are alive. Moto is curious that the two were taken to a hidden temple in the jungle, one that he very interested in as he has no record of it in any of his books and understands it to be an outstanding example of Khmer architecture. Moto also leads on that because he has not be able to obtain permission to explore it, the museum that he works for would pay very well for *any* information about it—even pictures of it. As freelance cameramen, this opportunity interests Marty but Chick is more interested in leaving the country—alive.

Before they separate, Mr. Moto shows them a poison dart shot from a blowgun—the murder weapon that killed the rajah's wife. In response to Marty's query how he knows this, Moto confesses that he knew this yesterday when he removed the dart from the wife's body after Marty and Chick were taken as prisoners by Bokor. Marty then damns Moto for knowing this information and allowing them to be nearly killed but Mr. Moto replies in a selfish but pragmatic tone, "I wish to keep my own head on my shoulders."

In the temple the next day, the guru relaxes knowing that Bokor is secretly watching him. He warns, "Bokor. Remember, my eyes can see through rocks as well as walls." The guru then admonishes the high priest that he does a poor job of guarding the temple, allowing strangers such as Mr. Moto to wander about and "dig up the graves of the ancient ones." Bokor informs the guru that he is powerless to do anything as Mr. Moto is protected by French authorities. According to Bokor, killing Mr. Moto would only bring down death and destruction at the hands of the white soldiers. Bokor then maneuvers to convince the guru himself to do away with Moto.

In the temple the guru discovers a secret cellar filled with explosives underneath the temple floor and goes down a ladder to investigate. One of Bokor's men sees the open door and draws closer to observe the guru below. Before he can pounce on and kill the old man, the guru pulls away, and after a brief scuffle, strangles the attacker dead. The guru then covers up all traces of the trap door and goes to another hidden room in the temple behind an idol where he removes his mask and reveals himself to be Mr. Moto. The Japanese agent again sends a message written in Japanese by carrier pigeon—this time writing that he has located the munitions base and that Bokor is the leader of the revolt.

As luck would have it, one of Rajah Ali's favorite pastimes is hunting with a shotgun. While shooting at birds that day, he shoots down the carrier pigeon boasting, "These foreign birds are not such difficult targets." When the dead pigeon is retrieved and brought to him, Rajah Ali sees the note Moto had written naming Bokor the leader of the revolt. He then vows, "When the time comes, Bokor will discover who is the stupid one!"

The rajah holds a celebration especially for Vicki that evening in which he plans to announce that, because of Keema's death, there is a "vacancy" in his harem. He is asking that Vicki become one of his many wives—to be called Rani Victoria I—a role which she accepts to Marty's surprise and disappointment. The rajah's subjects do not receive this news with much enthusiasm either.

In honor of his guests from "across the sea," Rajah Ali is proud to announce that he has had a truly Occidental dish prepared—each guest is served a bird shot down earlier by the rajah. However Mr. Moto receives an unexpected surprise—on his plate is the carrier pigeon with the note, concerning Bokor and the revolt, attached. On the other side of the note Rajah Ali added the message, "Thank you for interesting addition to menu." When Mr. Moto glances towards the rajah, the rajah happily smiles and chuckles.

Later that evening Mr. Moto is in his hut, adding the recently discovered hidden cellar with the explosives to a map of the temple he has drawn.

Hiding outside in the jungle is Bokor and two of his followers, one of whom Bokor then orders to kill Moto and then return to the temple. Having now completed the map, Mr. Moto rolls it up and hides it in a hollow tube. He then takes off his trademark steel-rimmed glasses to clean the lenses, and in its reflection, he sees that Bokor's henchman is about to attack him from behind with a knife. Moto is always vigilant and swiftly slays his attacker. Fearing that the hut may be watched by others, Moto assumes the identity of the dead native by putting on his clothes, leaves the hut, and heads into the jungle.

Bokor sees what he thinks is one of his followers leave the hut and now considers Moto dead. The high priest is curious as to what items are inside and enters the hut. While Bokor searches among Moto's belongings, Victoria Mason comes by. When she knocks on the door and calls out Mr. Moto's name, her presence scares off Bokor. Hearing no response from Mr. Moto, Vicki then enters the hut, looks among the hut's contents with Bokor now watching through the window, and easily finds the concealed map. On the map in the lower corner, she observes the notation, "Confidential Assignment A-61, K. Moto – 1937," revealing Mr. Moto to be on some sort of secret assignment while posing as an archaeologist.

Vicki then leaves the hut for the temple but is followed by Bokor and Yao. In the meanwhile from a distance, Chick sees Vicki heading towards the temple with Bokor behind her. He convinces Marty that Vicki is in danger and Marty rushes off to the temple. When Vicki reaches the temple grounds, she is seized and tied up by Bokor and Yao who want to know what her connection with Moto is. Even though she denies knowing anything, Bokor is unconvinced and is about to torture Vicki when Moto, again in disguise as the old guru, emerges from one of the temple's passages.

Bokor tells the guru that Vicki is an accomplice of Mr. Moto who is trying to interfere with his plan of leading a revolt against Rajah Ali. The guru then criticizes Bokor for the clumsy methods he uses in obtaining confessions and explains, "The wise ones teach ways of forcing the truth from unwilling lips." The guru then chants a mantra pretending to hypnotize Vicki. He draws close to Vicki and softly whispers that he is really Mr.

Clockwise from the upper left: Robert Kent, Rochelle Hudson, and Chick Chandler.

Moto and that she should pretend to sleep and answer *yes* to all his questions.

During the guru's interrogation of Vicki, Marty arrives at the temple. He punches the guru down but is then knocked unconscious and tied up by Yao. Bokor is then informed that a fire is burning down by the river, a signal that Capt. Zimmerman (Frederick Vogeding) has arrived to deliver munitions for Bokor's insurrection. Meanwhile, Chick is worried about Marty and heads for the temple when he sees the fires and Zimmerman's men. Thinking they are friendly, Chick goes to Zimmerman and asks his help in rescuing Marty and Vicki from Bokor.

When Zimmerman and Chick arrive at the temple, Bokor's men seize Chick. Mr. Moto, as the guru, asks what connection can Zimmerman, a white man, have with a high priest of Shiva. Bokor answers that Zimmerman has provided him with "certain necessary equipment" and when he is about to be paid for his delivery, Bokor has Yao impale Zimmerman with a spear.

"You paid him well," says Moto.

"He has served his purpose," replies Bokor in acknowledgment and then happily declares that his revolt against the weak rajah has now begun and it will not end until every foreigner is driven from Asia.

Bokor then orders Chick to be executed, but Vicki instinctively blurts out, "Mr. Moto, help him!" Bokor then realizes that the guru is really Moto. A fight then breaks out with Moto stabbing Yao and Bokor escaping. Moto, Vicki, Marty, and Chick now use the few guns Zimmerman had delivered to the temple to ward off Bokor's men.

By this time Mr. Moto has removed his disguise, and Vicki remarks that the guns and ammunition do not seem to be a surprise to him. Vicki also guesses that Mr. Moto had suspected that she was a secret agent of the British Intelligence Service from the beginning. Moto confides that she should have done a better job of hiding the flare to start the bogus fire in the airplane. Moto also confesses that he wanted her to find the hidden map of the temple and that he was on a mission to destroy Bokor's base of operations—the cellar with the explosives. The revelations that Vicki and Mr. Moto are both spies are big surprises to Marty and Chick

Just as Moto and his crew are about to run out of ammunition, Rajah Ali arrives with his loyal troops and captures Bokor and his followers. The rajah then badgers Bokor—"I too saw your signal fires Bokor, and I knew their meaning." He also brags that he knew that Bokor had his wife killed and that Zimmerman was bringing munitions. The monarch now promises that Bokor will die and he will use the same guns to restore the ancient kingdom of Tong Moi.

The rajah now turns to Mr. Moto and explains that because he is an excellent shot, none of his messages via carrier pigeon got through. Defeated, Moto admits to spying but insists Marty and Chick are not involved, a plea which the rajah does not accept—"Their mere presence here involves them."

Just when the rajah gives the orders to shoot the men, Vicki then rushes to the rajah and plays up to his vanity, expressing she had no idea how clever is the man she is about to marry. However this is simply a distraction for her unsuccessful attempt to grab a dagger from the rajah's belt. Meanwhile, Mr. Moto sneaks over to the door that leads to the cellar and threatens to blow them all up by dropping a torch into the room with the explosives if the rajah's men do not put down their guns. Rajah Ali, gun in hand, inches closer to Moto and calls his bluff—claiming that he would not dare to blow up his friends also. Mr. Moto stalls until Marty picks up a empty gun and throws it at the rajah's head, which causes the ruler to fall into the cellar.

Mr. Moto, Vicki, Marty, and Chick start to escape from the temple when Moto throws a lit torch at the rajah's soldiers. The torch ignites a fuse of movie film leading to the explosives which goes off when they are all clear of the temple.

The final scene on a sailboat has Marty affectionately involved with Vicki. Chick tells Marty that he is quitting the newsreel business as it is "too tough," and he is to become Mr. Moto's assistant. With tongue in cheek, Moto tests Chick's resolve by telling him that his next case involves a murderer of over 37 people who is reported to be on a small isolated volcanic island as the honored guest of a tribe of headhunters. When Moto asks Chick if the two of them should go and bring him back, Chick faints.

Commentary

This film never approaches the level of the series' first two films. Perhaps too many cooks spoiled the soup as there were two writers (Willis Cooper and Norman Foster) of the original story *and* two writers who collaborated on the screenplay (Lou Breslow and John Patrick). This combination results in a plot that, in author Richard Wires' words, "relied on the implausible and the melodramatic." If Mr. Moto was already working undercover to head off a planned revolt, why is it necessary to also have a British secret agent? The film also continues the formula, established in the series' previous entry, of having comic relief with actor Chick Chandler paired with Robert Kent serving as the straight man who is romantically attracted to Rochelle Hudson.

The review in *Variety* on June 15, 1938 warns that the fourth film in the series will be interesting only to fans of Peter Lorre, but it "Won't win new friends." The reviewer (Wear) comments on the film's collection of props:

> ". . . has trapdoors, poison air guns, hidden passages, machine guns, carrier pigeons, bolo knives, and a generous assortment of jungle beasts. There are too many hairbreadth escapes and uncanny accomplishments for a regulation feature. It all smacks of serial style."

The review also criticizes Lorre's dual role as Mr. Moto and a mysterious old guru, the latter which adds little to the plot other than to introduce a few cultural elements of Hindu mythology—Shiva and Naga.[31] Even the jungle setting is uninspiring, which caused B. R. Crisler's *New York Times* review of June 13, 1938 to pan Albert Hogsett's art direction, lam-

---

31   Shiva is one of the two principal Hindu gods—the other being Vishnu. Shiva is frequently viewed as the destroyer of the world prior to each period of devastation. *Naga* is Hindi for "divine serpent." The term denotes a race of supernatural aquatic beings according to Hindu mythology and are considered the keepers of fertility. The king of them is Sesha, the sacred serpent of the god Vishnu.

pooning the geographical French Indochina as "Indoor China." Other than the performers and the effective makeup that transforms Moto into a wrinkled, old guru, there was clearly not much else to recommend about the film.

Film Notes

The working title of *Mr. Moto Takes a Chance* is *Look Out, Mr. Moto*, whose production began on July 19, 1937. Although this was intended to be the second film of the *Mr. Moto* series, it was not released until June 24, 1938, when it was the fourth film of the series. In its issue of August 5, 1937, a *Hollywood Reporter* news item mentioned that the production of *Mr. Moto Takes a Chance* would be held up temporarily while the studio watches the developments of the Sino-Japanese War. The news item also noted that because the leading character is a Japanese, the script may have to be overhauled to avoid injured feelings.

Based on the history and geography of the region, which is somewhere in Laos, the film is somewhat accurate. Stock footage of Ankor Wat is mixed in to set the geographic locale.[32] In the protectorates of French Indochina (Laos, Cambodia, and Vietnam), the French ruled indirectly through native officials. In the film, Rajah Ali explains that, as ruler of his small kingdom, his limited power is granted by the French. The map in the film's introductory scene shows the kingdom of Tong Moi just below the region known as Luang Prahbang. The French actually had a native monarch for Laos but he was to rule only Luang Prahbang, the ancient capital of the Lan Xang Kingdom. However, the Tong Moi of the film is fictitious.

---

32   Angkor, in northwest Cambodia (now Khmer Republic), was the great capital city of the Khmer empire from the city's founding in about 880 until about 1225. Once lost in the jungle for centuries, it was discovered by French missionaries in the 1860s. Angkor Wat, meaning Angkor Temple, is the greatest of Angkor's temple complexes and is larger in scale than the Egyptian pyramids. The temple compound was designed as a dwelling for the deified spirit of a dead king and covers an area of 4,920 by 4,265 feet and is surrounded by a 590-foot wide moat.

According to the studio's pressbook for the film, director Norman Foster insisted that the characters speak Cambodian. To insure accuracy in the language, the studio hired Louis Vincenot, who was born in Cambodia, to teach the language to the extras. The pressbook also indicates that Rochelle Hudson wore authentic Cambodian gowns and jewelry in the film. Incidentally, Peter Lorre would again appear with Rochelle Hudson in *Island of Doomed Men* (1940), one of his first films after the *Mr. Moto* series.

Mysterious Mr. Moto (1938)

Twentieth Century-Fox Film Corp. Distributed by Twentieth Century-Fox Film Corp. Released: October 21, 1938; New York opening: September 17, 1938. Production: March 21 to mid-April 1938. Copyright Twentieth Century-Fox Film Corp., October 21, 1938; LP8599. Sound: Western Electric Mirrophonic Recording. B&W. 7 reels. 5,672 feet. 63 minutes. PCA certificate number 4213.

Executive producer: Sol M. Wurtzel. Director: Norman Foster. Original screen play: Philip MacDonald and Norman Foster, based on the character "Mr. Moto" created by John. P. Marquand. Photography: Virgil Miller, A.S.C. Art direction: Bernard Herzbrun and Lewis Creber. Film editor: Norman Colbert. Costumes: Herschel. Sound: Joseph E. Aiken and William H. Anderson. Musical direction: Samuel Kaylin. Assistant directors: Jasper Blystone* and Charles Faye.* Camera operator: L.B. Abbott.* Assistant cameraman: Ted Weisbarth.* Gaffer: Fred Hall.* Assistant cutter: Douglas Biggs.* Set dresser: Walter Scott.* Wardrobe girl: Le Vaughn Larson.* Wardrobe man: Sandy Sandeen.* Assistant sound: C.J. Mazzoletti.* Boom man: Harry Roberts.* Cable man: Fred Casey.* Hair stylist: Wilma Ryan.* Makeup: Ben Nye.* Production manager: Ed. Ebele.* Unit manager: Ben Wurtzel.* Script clerk: Rose Steinberg.* Grip: Roger Murphy.* Assistant grip: Harry Jones.* Props: Don Greenwood.* Assistant prop men: Stinley Detlie* and Monroe Liebgoid.* Best boy: John Grady.* Casting: Virgil Hart.* Still photographer: Tad Gillum.* Publicity: Harry Brand.* Stunts: Harvey Perry* and Billy Jones.*

Songs: *It's the Same, the Whole World Over*, music and lyrics by John Paul Lock Barton and Bert Massee; *Black Black Sheep*, music by Louis De Francesco, lyrics by Frank Tuttle.

Cast

Peter Lorre *as* . . . . Mr. [Kentaro] Moto [alias Ito Matsuka]
Mary Maguire . . . . Ann Richman
Henry Wilcoxon . . . . Anton Darvak
Erik Rhodes . . . . David Scott-Frensham
Harold Huber . . . . Ernst Litmar
Leon Ames . . . . Paul Brissac [alias Mr. Romero]
Forrester Harvey . . . . George Higgins
Fredrik Vogeding . . . . Gottfried Brujo
Lester Matthews . . . . Sir Charles Murchison
John Rogers . . . . Sniffy
Karen Sorrell . . . . Lotus Liu
Mitchell Lewis . . . . Nola
Frank S Hagney* . . . . Commissionaire
Barney O'Toole* . . . . Tough
Val Slanton* . . . . Organ grinder
Ernie Stanton* . . . . Sidewalk artist
Colin Kenny,* Cyril Thornton* . . . . Phony policemen
William Austin* . . . . Artist
Harry Depp* . . . . Little man
Evelyn Beresford* . . . . Large English woman
Pat O'Malley,* Leyland Hodgson* . . . . Police sergeants
Kenneth Hunter* . . . . Superintendent Murray
Dick Rush* . . . . Constable
Bruce Sydney,* Les Sketchley,* Paul McVey* . . . . . Plainclothesmen
Clive Morgan* . . . . Secretary
Major Sam Harris* . . . . Lord Gilford
Cecil Weston* . . . . Bartender
Tiny Jones* . . . . Flower woman
James Kilgannon,* Yorke Sherwood,* Harry Allen* . . . . . Taxi drivers
Reginald Barlow* . . . . Policeman
Dave Thursby* . . . . Truck driver
Jimmy Aubrey* . . . . Newsboy
Clyde Cook* . . . . Sandwich man
May Beatty* . . . . Woman at inquiry
Herbert Evans* . . . . Constable
Major George C. McBride* . . . . Trick coin expert

Adia Kuznetzoff* . . . . Freighter captain
Billy Bevan* . . . . Customs official
Noble Johnson* . . . . Native sergeant
Eugene Borden* . . . . Radio announcer
Charles Bennett* . . . . Cockney singer
Norman Foster* . . . . Hoodlum in tavern
Leonard Mudie* . . . . Monk

---

*Unbilled

"Softly, Softly, Catchee Monkey"
—Sign on Sir Charles Murchison's desk

The Story

The film's action opens with Mr. Moto and Paul Brissac (Leon Ames)
making their escape from the French penal colony of Devil's Island in
South America. Moto is posing as Ito Matsuka who was convicted of manslaughter in Saigon. Together and without any weapons, they elude track-
ing dogs, prison guards, and Indian natives as they flee through the jungles
of French Guiana. They finally make their way to a small river where Moto
has hidden a canoe and they paddle for three days until they arrive at Cayenne where Brissac pays a freighter captain (Adia Kuznetzoff) 20,000 francs
to provide him and Moto with fresh clothes and passage to Lisbon. From
there, Brissac plans to go alone to London but Moto wants to go too,
saying Brissac will need a Number One houseboy there. Brissac at first dismisses the suggestion—figuring he will find a houseboy there—but Moto
convinces Brissac boasting, "Not like Ito. Cleaning immense; cooking pretentious; cocktails supreme. Pleasing you?"

Proceeding down the gangway at the London docks, Moto and Brissac
are met by George Higgins (Forrester Harvey), a talkative lawyer who
addresses Brissac as "Mr. Romero." Brissac easily clears customs with a
forged passport and diplomatic visa while Moto's passport identifies him

as Ito Takau. Brissac then quietly asks Higgins if our "branch manager" has made suitable arrangements for him. The lawyer responds that he has found a quiet apartment for Brissac in London's West End on Half Moon Street. Apparently Brissac's arrival in London had been expected after his successful escape from Devil's Island.

A few days later, Higgins and an associate, Ernst Litmar (Harold Huber), visit Brissac's apartment to discuss Brissac's future role in London. To warm things up first, Higgins suggests that they have one of Ito's special drinks, one which Ito has suitably christened as "Memories of St. Joseph." This name however is lost on Higgins as he does not understand its significance. Brissac then explains to Higgins that St. Joseph, from Ito's perspective, has nothing to do with being religious, but is the name of a windowless prison far away.

Despite Brissac's utmost confidence in Ito, Litmar nevertheless is suspicious of the houseboy. Higgins brags, "Ito's all right, as soon as you get used to his face. He's one of us, he is. He's the one who got Mr. Romero . . ." and is then cut short by Litmar with the strict admonition that he talks too much.

To avoid being overheard, Litmar then recommends Brissac have Ito take the rest of the day off. Litmar then reveals the true nature of their business—they are all part of a organization, called the "League of Assassins" and kills for hire. Litmar tells Brissac that his first assignment is a man named Anton Darvak who is currently in London and whom Brissac remembers as "The Steel King of Prague."

At his suite at the Park Lane Hotel, Darvak (Henry Wilcoxon) is seen combining his company's business with pleasure—dictating items to his secretary Ann Richman (Mary Maguire) and playing Chopin on the piano. He then receives a threatening telephone call which is secretly overheard by Ann on another phone from one of the League's henchmen, a man named Sniffy (John Rogers). Sniffy reminds Darvak that he has ignored previous warnings over the past several months but is now given a deadline of three o'clock on the following day to part with his steel formula or be killed. To show that they mean business, Darvak will be given a final warning later that afternoon. After Darvak hangs up, he is visited by David Scott-

Frensham (Erik Rhodes), a business associate who, along with Ann, is concerned about the death threat. Darvak however seems unfazed.

Mr. Moto, now *sans* disguise, stops by Scotland Yard to see Sir Charles Murchison (Lester Matthews), an old acquaintance who is chief of the Yard's Criminal Investigation Division. As a member of the International Police, Moto tells Sir Charles that he is obliged to report his presence in London to hunt down the League of Assassins. Murchison however finds it difficult to believe hired killers are in London but nevertheless offers whatever assistance the Yard can provide, an offer Moto declines for time being.

When asked about what proof Moto has that the gang is in London, Moto reminds Sir Charles about Brissac and the Japanese fellow that escaped with him from Devil's Island. Murchison now realizes it was Mr. Moto who went undercover and engineered the escape, hoping to be led to the rest of the gang. Moto says he now knows most of them but is still seeking the identity of the group's leader and the reason for their presence in London. Despite Sir Charles' eagerness to bring in the known individuals, Moto declines to provide any further information, reminding Murchison of a sign on his own desk—"Softly, Softly, Catchee Monkey."

After leaving Scotland Yard, Mr. Moto manages to elude the two detectives Sir Charles ordered to follow Moto and find out where he lives. Now back in disguise as Ito, Moto then takes a cab to the Limehouse causeway where he enters The Blue Peter, a seedy cockney pub that serves as a gathering place for the thugs who work for the League of Assassins. Once inside, Moto strikes up a conversation with Lotus Liu (Karen Sorrell), a Eurasian who Sniffy calls the "mystery lady." However, Moto's presence has not gone unnoticed and being a foreigner, is made to feel unwelcomed by Sniffy and several patrons.

Lotus then leads Moto to her apartment above the tavern where it becomes clear that she is Mr. Moto's undercover agent in London and has quietly observed the activities of certain people. She tells Mr. Moto that Sniffy works for Higgins who has been secretive whenever she tried to press him for information but earlier overheard Sniffy telephoning a man at the Park Lane Hotel, one with a strange name—Darvak. Mr. Moto is surprised at this revelation as he knows Anton Darvak to be a steel industrialist and guesses that Darvak may be the reason for the group's business in London.

Traveling in a cab to visit Darvak, Mr. Moto is caught in a traffic jam in an outdoor market. Suddenly the organ grinder changes the tune he is playing to "*Madrid*," the cue for the driver of a lorry[33] to back up and intentionally run over a man. Moto witnesses the horrific event but initially attaches no significance to it. The police conclude from eyewitnesses that the death was accidental.

Mr. Moto arrives at Darvak's hotel room and informs the steel maker that he is from the International Police and is offering any assistance regarding the threat on his life. Darvak at first refuses to tell Moto about the threat against his life despite the urgings of Ann Richman and David Scott-Frensham. Moto then observes a painting by an artist named Garnot that Darvak is considering purchasing. David then brags to Mr. Moto that Anton has a weakness for Garnot; Moto also confesses that he has also admired the painter's work. Pleased to meet a fellow art connoisseur,

33 British term for a motor truck.

Leon Ames and Peter Lorre make their way through the jungle in their escape from Devil's Island.

Darvak tells Mr. Moto that he might be interested in an exhibition being held at the Coventry Galleries the next day which also features a painting by Garnot.

Just then, Brissac telephones Anton Darvak to inform him that his friend Lord Gilford (Major Sam Harris) has met with a serious accident. He was knocked down by a lorry and died instantly—killed as the promised warning to Darvak. The steel magnate then confides to Mr. Moto that he was told he would be killed the next afternoon at three o'clock if he does not part with his steel formula but still refuses to be intimidated. Scott-Frensham suggests that Darvak have Scotland Yard protect him but Darvak is still not convinced. After Moto leaves, Darvak and David are nevertheless suspicious of Mr. Moto. Although both have heard of Moto, neither has ever seen him and for all they know, the man claiming to be Moto could be one of the assassins.

At the Limehouse tavern Higgins meets up with Lotus Liu and joins her at a table with a drink. In response to her asking him about his "connections," Higgins begins to talk. Unknown to Higgins however, Monk (Leonard Mudie), another of the League's henchmen, overhears the talkative lawyer and sneaks out to telephone an unknown superior, reporting that Higgins is talking considerably. Monk hangs up after acknowledging, "I think that can be arranged."

Mr. Moto, again disguised as Ito, enters the pub and makes a subtle signal to Lotus, and then sits at a distant table. David Scott-Frensham has followed Moto to the pub and cautiously enters so that he is not seen by Moto. Monk returns and talks to the bartender, Sniffy, and a few other thugs, one of whom then goes over to the accordion player, drops a coin into a tin can, and whispers something in his ear as if making a request for a particular song. Suddenly, the music changes to *"Madrid,"* the same melody the organ grinder played immediately before Lord Gilford was killed. Hearing the music, Higgins is petrified—he knows its meaning and wants to leave. But before he can, a staged fight breaks out. Moto rushes to Lotus and both head to her room for safety. In the stairway they find Higgins' dead body—"He was told that he talked too much," Moto remarks. Moto tells Lotus that she must escape and never come back to the tavern as she is now in danger because Higgins confided in her.

At Brissac's residence Ernst Litmar stops by and first tells Brissac that Mr. Higgins has "resigned" from the organization. Next, Litmar reveals that Ito is really Mr. Moto of the International Police and that he arranged to be in prison and escape with Brissac to win his confidence. To deal with Moto, Litmar orders Brissac that, when Moto returns, he is to be sent to a store on Gladstone street as an excuse to purchase some fruit as necessary ingredients for brandy cups Litmar has promised to make. There, Litmar knows that Mr. Moto will find "matters arranged for him."

Moto arrives at the given location and he hears a blind street violinist suddenly play the same tune he heard immediately before the two previous murders. Now proceeding with caution, Mr. Moto is soon confronted by several street thugs alongside a cab, but Moto uses his ju-jitsu skills to handle the assailants and escapes in the cab.

Early the next day Mr. Moto goes to the Coventry Galleries, knowing that Anton Darvak plans to be there that afternoon at three o'clock to see the art exhibition. Unseen in an upper balcony, Moto overhears Litmar tell Brissac and Gottfried Brujo (Fredrik Vogeding), another gang member who has arranged the art show, the details of his plan to kill Darvak. Although Litmar has been ordered not to be at the exhibition, he says that their leader will position Darvak in front of a particular painting directly underneath a massive chandelier. Because no one other than Litmar knows the identity of their leader, the plan has the leader calling Darvak's name in a loud voice as the signal for Brujo to have the orchestra play the *Madrid* death melody. Brissac, hiding in the gallery's loft, will then break the chandelier's chain when he hears the musical cue and its fall will kill the industrialist.

Meanwhile, Ann Richman still questions her boss's insistence about going to the art exhibition that afternoon. In frustration she tells the surprised Darvak that she loves him and that he would have known her feelings months ago if he wasn't so preoccupied with his steel business—a confession Darvak is pleased to hear.

Mr. Moto then visits Darvak and the steel maker apologizes for his suspicion that the Japanese was part of the murder ring. Ann adds that

David Scott-Frensham knows someone at Scotland Yard and found out all about the famous Mr. Moto. Coincidentally, David now arrives and says that he has brought two men from Scotland Yard to protect Darvak wherever he goes. Moto approves of David's action and then tries to recall who might have said, "The best way to avoid death is not to have too much aversion to it." David replies that it sounds like Schopenhauer.[34]

The telephone rings and the call is for Mr. Moto. On the other end is the Limehouse tavern bartender (Cecil Weston) who tries to trick Moto by giving him a message that his lady friend needs help and the gang has her. Moto is also told he might be able to save her if he returns to the tavern. Moto excuses himself and is met in the hallway outside Darvak's hotel room by two men posing as detectives from Scotland Yard who say they have orders to "bring him in." As luck would have it, one of the men drops a gun and Moto realizes that the men are part of a trap as Scotland Yard policemen do not carry guns. He again uses his martial arts skills to throw the two assailants down the staircase and makes his escape.

At the gallery, Brujo, Sniffy, and Monk take turns guessing who their unknown superior might be from those in attendance. All of a sudden, a

cantankerous artist loudly complains in German about the quality of the exhibit—an insult to the name of art, he exclaims. Brujo, also in German, asks the artist what is troubling him and threatens to throw him out. The artist counters that he has paid for his admission to the show and can't be removed but Brujo warns him to behave himself nonetheless. Monk and Brujo then wonder if the artist could be their leader in disguise.

At Scotland Yard, Lotus Liu strives to convince Sir Charles Murchison that Mr. Moto now needs his help at the art gallery and also pleads for him to hurry because Mr. Darvak maybe arriving at the gallery right now. Ernst Litmar, now being held in police custody, threatens to sue for false arrest but Lotus begs the CID chief not to release Litmar until they visit the gallery, after which he'll have his proof.

As three o'clock nears, David Scott-Frensham arrives at the gallery and goes towards the irritable artist who is still complaining in German about the quality of the artwork on exhibit. Standing directly under the chandelier, the artist then pleads with David.

"I know you're a patron of the arts, Mr. Darvak! I'm a good painter Mr. Darvak! Please help me Mr. Darvak!"

Upon hearing the signal, Brujo nervously signals the orchestra to play the death melody. David is shocked at both being called "Darvak" and hearing the all-too-familiar tune. Brissac, also hearing the music, on cue strikes the chain supporting the chandelier with a sledge hammer. As the chandelier falls, the artist is quick to get out of the way but David is killed instantly.

Darvak and Ann arrive to see the chandelier fall on David. They rush to the body but Darvak says David is dead. The artist then removes his disguise and reveals himself to be Mr. Moto, who took the liberty of pretending that David was Anton Darvak, as David was the ring leader of the League of Assassins. Sir Charles then arrives on the scene to congratulate Moto who correctly deduced that the chandelier would be the murder weapon at the gallery. Mr. Moto further explains he knew that the leader must be David because David knew all of Darvak's moves and the phony Scotland Yard detectives carrying guns were provided by David.

Sir Charles remarks, "So we now have a whole cage full of monkeys which Mr. Moto promised us." Moto corrects Sir Charles as Brissac is still missing. Murchison's attention is then drawn towards the ceiling where Brissac is just about to fire a shot. As Sir Charles warns everyone to get back, he is shot in the shoulder. Moto then races up to the building's loft to apprehend Brissac. After a lengthy fight, Moto subdues Brissac and yells to Sir Charles to send up three policemen to the loft. Murchison asks if Moto captured Brissac. Moto affirms, "Catchee monkey, but not so softly."

Commentary

Mysterious Mr. Moto is a marked improvement over the series' previous entry, *Mr. Moto Takes a Chance*. Even though much of the story is commonplace and the dialog might be improved a bit, the film does deliver lots of action, an ingredient that helped make the first two films of the series successful. One has to look very carefully during the film as director Norman Foster himself portrays the role of a hoodlum for the brawl scene in the Limehouse tavern.

The comic relief which had contributed to the disappointment of both *Mr. Moto's Gamble* and *Mr. Moto Takes a Chance* is now absent, allowing the viewer now to concentrate on the film as an action-packed adventure. The reviewer for *Variety* (Flin) in his June 1, 1938 review wrote, "The mystery of the 'Mysterious Mr. Moto' is why the formula isn't used more frequently in more pretentious productions. No one ever walks out on them."

The London setting seems to agree better with director Norman Foster than the *faux* jungles of the previous film. The atmosphere of the city's seedy Limehouse district allows for "Characters in this latest of the Moto series are Dickenesque in appearance and diction" (*Variety*).

As a whodunit, the identity of the ring leader of the League of Assassins is not much of a secret by the time the film is half over. Erik Rhodes portrays a similar snob in his role as Max Corday in *Charlie Chan in Paris*. Nonetheless, the writers save much of their best suspense and action for the film's ending. Moto nonchalantly allows a falling chandelier to kill the ring leader and Moto's capture of Brissac is perhaps the best fight scene of the entire *Mr. Moto* series.

One interesting note for those who have watched the series from the start, is the progressive elevation of Mr. Moto from the director of an importing firm, to a confidential detective for the International Association of Importers, and then to the rank of "agent general" of the International Police—number 673.

Film Notes

The film, *Mysterious Mr. Moto* went into production on March 21, 1938 under the working title of *Mysterious Mr. Moto of Devil's Island* and was released seven months later on October 21 as the last of three *Mr. Moto* films to be released that year. Actor Michael Whalen was originally cast for the role of Anton Darvak but he was needed for his role as Matt Kerry in *Speed to Burn* (1938). Whalen was replaced by Henry Wilcoxon who had previously portrayed Marc Antony in Cecille B. DeMille's 1934 version of *Cleopatra*.

Twentieth Century-Fox purchased twenty feet of stock footage entitled "Chase Through Devil's Island", from Columbia Pictures for use in this film. Author Jon Tuska in his book, *The Detective in Hollywood*, recalls one anecdote relayed by Leon Ames about the film's production. While he and Lorre were crawling into a small boat during their escape from Devil's Island and being shot at, director Norman Foster had sharpshooters on the set out on the Fox back lot using *real* bullets!

One nice carryover from several of the previous films in the series is the use of geographic references. Several are related to Brissac's and Moto's escape: Devil's Island, a noted French penal colony in South America,[35] their arrival in French Guiana's capital, Cayenne,[36] and the cocktail called,

---

35 Cayenne is the capital and main port of French Guiana.

36 Devil's Island (Île du Diable) is part of the French overseas department of French Guiana and is the smallest and southernmost of the three Îles du Salut

(Salvation Islands). The island is located in the Atlantic Ocean about eight
Clockwise from the upper left: Henry Wilcoxon, Erik Rhodes, Leon Ames,
and Harold Huber. Devil's Island was used largely for political prisoners, the most cele-
brated of whom was Alfred Dreyfus. The notoriously brutal penal colonies

"Memories of St. Joseph," a coded reference to a prison on St. Joseph's Island.

Even in London, there are several reasonably accurate references to locations and buildings. Brissac's apartment on Half Moon Street is actually a street in the Mayfair section of London's West End across from James Park on Piccadilly. Limehouse is a district in London's East End on the Thames and was originally the first Chinatown of London. In Victorian times, the Limehouse district had a colorful reputation as a mass of opium dens and illegal gambling joints but is now inhabited largely by sailors and dockworkers. Gladstone Street, where Litmar tells his houseboy Ito to get some fruit from is a street near the Newington section in southeast London, but it is quite a distance from Brissac's apartment. As for Anton Darvak's hotel, the Park Lane Hotel, it was built in 1932 and is on Piccadilly overlooking Green Park. In fact, the hotel is right around the corner from the location of Brissac's fictitious apartment on Half Moon Street.

---

were phased out between 1938 and 1951.

Peter LORRE
Mr. MOTO'S LAST WARNING
Ricardo CORTEZ
Virginia FIELD
John CARRADINE
George SANDERS
Joan CAROL
SOL M. WURTZEL
Norman Foster
A 20th CENTURY FOX PICTURE

Mr. Moto's Last Warning (1939)

Twentieth Century-Fox Film Corp. Distributed by Twentieth Century-Fox Film Corp. Released: January 20, 1939. Production: June 6 to June 29, 1938. Sound: Western Electric Mirrophonic Recording. B&W. 7 reels. 6,376 feet. 71 minutes. PCA certificate number 4445.

Executive producer: Sol M. Wurtzel. Director: Norman Foster. Original screen play: Philip MacDonald and Norman Foster, based on the character "Mr. Moto" created by John P. Marquand. Photography: Virgil Miller, A.S.C. Art direction: Bernard Herzbrun, Lewis Creber, and Freddie Stoos.* Set decoration: Thomas Little. Film editor: Norman Colbert. Costumes: Helen A. Myron. Sound: E. Clayton Ward and William H. Anderson. Musical direction: Samuel Kaylin. Assistant directors: Jasper Blystone* and Charles Faye.* Camera operator: William Whitley.* Assistant cameramen: Jack Warren.* Gaffer: L.V. Johnson.* Assistant cutter: Doug Biggs.* Set dresser: Walter Scott.* Assistant prop men: Larry Haddock* and Walter Poggi.* Wardrobe man: Sandy Sandeen.* Assistant sound: Emmet O'Brien.* Boom man: Harry Roberts.* Hair stylist: Jean Thomas.* Make-up: Fred Phillips.* Production manager: V.L. McFadden.* Unit manager: Sam Schneider.* Script clerk: Helen Torres.* Grip: Roger Murphy.* Assistant grip: Dan Wurtzel.* Props: George Peckham.* Casting: Phillip Moore.* Best boy: F. Mime.* Cable man: M. Braggins.* Still photographer: Tad Gillum*

Cast

Peter Lorre *as*. . . . . Mr. Moto [alias, H. Kuroki]
Ricardo Cortez . . . . Fabian [the Great]
Virginia Field . . . . Connie [Porter]
John Carradine. . . . . Danforth [alias for Richard Burke]
George Sanders . . . . Eric Norvel
Joan Carol . . . . Mary Delacour
Robert Coote . . . . Rollo [Venables]
Margaret Irving . . . . Madame Delacour
Leyland Hodgson. . . . . [Capt. Burt] Hawkins
John Davidson . . . . Hakim
Teru Shimada*. . . . . Fake Mr. Moto
Georges Renavent* . . . . Admiral Delacour
E.E. Clive* . . . . Commandant
Holmes Herbert* . . . . Bentham
C. Montague Shaw* . . . . First Lord of Admiralty
George Humbert* . . . . Stage manager
Jacques Lory* . . . . Cliquot the juggler
Dennis D'Auburn* . . . . Deck officer
Eric Wilton* . . . . Deck steward
Jimmy Aubrey* . . . . Waiter
Lal Chand Mehra* . . . . Customs officer
Victor Metzetti* . . . . Cab driver
Bert Roach* . . . . Hotel clerk
Jack Perry* . . . . Mug
A. R. Bogard* . . . . Hoist man
Wayne Rivers* . . . . Cable man
Daniel Boone,* Al Wesslen* . . . . Deep sea divers
H. W. Stroele,* Robert F. Owens* . . . . Tenders
Neil Fitzgerald*. . . . . English sergeant

---

*Unbilled

"Judo often miscall by foreigners ju-jitsu."
—H. Kuroki to Rollo Venables

The Story

The British First Lord of Admiralty (C. Montague Shaw) has just been notified that a French fleet has left Tunis and is heading towards the Egyptian city of Port Said to participate in joint sea maneuvers with them in the Red Sea. Bentham (Holmes Herbert), a British secret service officer, informs the admiral that he received information of a possible plot to disrupt peaceful relations between the two powers and inquires if they can detain the French fleet until they receive additional information from their agents. The admiral says that he'll talk to the prime minister to request a delay in the fleet's arrival for a few days.

The scene shifts to aboard the *S.S. Himalaya* where Madame Delacour (Margaret Irving) is traveling with her little daughter Mary (Joan Carol). Joining them on deck is Eric Norvel (George Sanders), a suave, mustachioed continental type who wears a monocle. At a time when Europe is bordering on war with the Axis Powers, Norvel is part of a sabotage ring plotting to upset British-French relations. The ship has just docked in Port Said and moments before they are about to go ashore, Madame Delacour receives a radiogram from her husband Admiral Delacour (Georges Renavent), the commander of the French fleet. He writes her that his arrival at Port Said will be delayed three days longer than planned.

Seeing the expression on her face as she reads the message, Norvel asks Madame Delacour if the message contains any bad news, to which she replies that the news is only "disappointing." Novel tries to pump the admiral's wife further, mentioning that he hopes that the maneuvers haven't been called off, but she cautiously responds that there are only a change of orders.

"It must be very interesting to receive important information like that before anyone else," says the spy.

Madame Delacour jokes, "Admirals' wives are always the last to hear anything of real importance."

Joining them in conversation is a bumbling Englishman named Rollo Venables (Robert Coote) who is collecting ideas from his travels for a novel he hopes to write. Mary asks the amateur adventurer if she is in his book and Rollo responds that everyone is in the book, even the Oriental sherlock.

"What's a sherlock?" Mary inquires.

"He means Monsieur Moto, darling," answers her mother.

With the sudden mention of Moto's name, Norvel then wonders where Mr. Moto is, for he wants to say goodbye to him. A Japanese (Teru Shimada) masquerading as Mr. Moto unexpectedly appears and tells Norvel that there is no need for good-byes as he will be staying with friends in Port Said for several days before traveling on.

On his way to retrieve his baggage, the man masquerading as Mr. Moto intentionally bumps into the real Mr. Moto. After excusing himself, Mr. Moto hands the undercover agent a message written in Japanese—"Will call you tomorrow. Continue to watch Norvel. Moto." Cautious, the Moto pretender then swallows the paper.

Norvel is sitting in his cab and then instructs the driver to just miss hitting the Japanese agent. Norvel quickly exits the cab and after seeing the pretend Mr. Moto is unhurt, apologizes profusely and insists that he be allowed to give the Japanese a ride. The pretend Mr. Moto is apprehensive but nonetheless gets into the cab, but soon realizes that he is being taken to an area he does not recognize. He is ordered to get out of the cab and when led into a building, is quickly murdered.

Later, Norvel meets up with Madame Delacour and Rollo in the lounge of the Khedive Hotel. Rollo is looking for some adventure and mentions that they should see the *real* Port Said, not the tourists traps. Norvel declines Rollo's invitation, claiming he has a prior business meeting scheduled. A man named Hakim (John Davidson), who wears a fez, arrives and tells Norvel he has a very urgent message for him. He hands Norvel a piece of paper which is a program for the acts at the Sultana Theatre of Variety. For some reason Norvel's eyes then focus on the title of the third act—*Fabian the Great, Ventriloquist Extraordinary.* Norvel then mentions his appointment has been canceled and suggests that they be his guests at the local music hall tonight.

At the Sultana Theatre with Norvel and Madame Delacour, Rollo is enjoying himself while watching a ventriloquist named Fabian (Ricardo Cortez) perform his act with his dummy, Alf. Sitting in different locations in the audience are the real Mr. Moto and Richard Burke (John Carradine), a bearded British secret agent posing as a man named Danforth who has infiltrated the sabotage ring.

An intermission follows Fabian's act and Norvel excuses himself from Madame Delacour on the pretext of going to smoke a cigarette. At the same time Burke and Hakim also head backstage and all are secretly followed by Mr. Moto. They meet with Fabian in his dressing room while Mr. Moto sneaks into the dressing room next to Fabian's. There, he inserts an amplifier with microphone through the room's air vent to better hear what is being said by Fabian and his associates in the next room.

Fabian tells his associates that it was probably no coincidence that Norvel and Mr. Moto were traveling on the same boat to Port Said but Norvel took care of Moto. Fabian also cautions that they must be careful not reveal what country is behind the plot. Norvel adds that he still hasn't gotten the exact arrival date of the French fleet but is still trying.

The ventriloquist then reveals a small notebook which he proudly says is his version of a police rogue's gallery—pictures and brief descriptions of government agents, information which took him years to compile. Fabian turns to the page reserved for Mr. Moto, which describes him as a member of the International Police but it has no photograph. Fabian then takes a pencil and makes a big "X" on the page—"So much for Mr. Moto," Fabian sneers.

Danforth is interested in seeing the book and after thumbing through several pages, is horrified to see a page with his own picture, *sans* beard, and his true identity as Richard Burke: British Secret Service Agent S-14. As Danforth, Burke tries to press Fabian for more details about the plot but Fabian tells him, "You'll know in plenty of time."

Just as they are about to leave his dressing room, Fabian thinks he hears a noise although Norvel and Danforth claim they hear nothing. Just to make sure though, Fabian decides to check the dressing room next to his, which belongs to Cliquot (Jacques Lory), a juggler whose act includes a small dog. When Fabian opens the door, he sees Moto, disguised as the juggler in a clown costume with makeup, practicing juggling.

However, when they leave the dressing room and head towards the stage, Fabian sees Cliquot performing his act on the stage and now realizes that an impostor was in the dressing room and may have overheard their sabotage plans. They go back to the clown's dressing room and finding it empty, split up to search the theater. During this time, Burke sneaks back to Fabian's dressing room and just when he is about to tear out the page with his picture from Fabian's notebook, Moto comes out from hiding and convinces Burke that it would be unwise to do so. Mr. Moto reveals who he is and gives Burke the address of an Oriental curio shop where Burke is to meet him later.

In the meanwhile, Norvel returns to his seat and seeing Madame Delacour's purse open with the radiogram inside, stealthily removes it, and places it in his coat pocket. Fabian returns to his dressing room and finds

Virginia Field, Peter Lorre, and Ricardo Cortez.

his notebook has been tampered with—someone had started to tear a page from his notebook it but stopped. Fabian opens the book to the page belonging to Richard Burke and stares at the picture for a moment. On a hunch, he then takes a pencil and draws a beard on Burke's photo. Fabian then smiles, turns to his dummy, and shows him the picture asking Alf if Mr. Burke looks like Danforth.

Following his performance, Fabian goes to Connie's Place, a seedy bar run by his girlfriend Connie Porter (Virginia Field), where he rents a room upstairs. Connie makes it known she is sick of Alf and whatever business Fabian is in. She peppers her boyfriend with a barrage of questions. Why does she have to run a dive? Why does she have to pretend that she hardly knows Fabian? Why can't they be together more? Why does he work in a third-rate music hall? All this is too much for Fabian who then agrees to tell Connie about everything.

Meanwhile, Burke pays a late visit to the Oriental antique shop across the street from Connie's Place which Mr. Moto operates as a front with the alias of H. Kuroki. Once inside Burke tells Mr. Moto he thought the Japanese agent was dead, mentioning that Fabian usually does not make mistakes. Moto then informs the British agent that the murdered man who deliberately posed as him was a colleague assigned to keep Norvel under observation while he in turn poses as an Oriental art dealer. Burke confesses the only information he was able to pass onto his superiors was that there was a plot to cause trouble between England and France and it had an unknown connection with the French fleet.

Norvel now enters Connie's Place and is met by Hawkins (Leyland Hodgson), the skipper of the *Vulcan*, a salvage vessel, who tells Norvel that Fabian is upstairs waiting for him. When they meet, Fabian introduces Connie to Norvel and after Connie leaves the room, Fabian warns Norvel not to talk in front of her. "If you have to, we're in the smuggling rackets," is the excuse he told Connie because she was getting too curious.

Norvel mentions he finally had a chance to read the radiogram Madame Delacour received but it didn't specify the fleet's arrival date. Fabian is disappointed and reminds Norvel that it is important they know when the fleet will arrive and fears they are being watched. Norvel is glad they got rid of Mr. Moto but Fabian has lingering doubts about who the man was in the theater posing as the juggler. In addition, Fabian then shows Norvel his notebook of government agents, pointing out the picture of Burke now with the penciled-in beard. The ventriloquist adds that someone was in his dressing room that evening and started to tear out that page but stopped. Norvel sees the photo resembles Danforth but replies that Danforth couldn't possibly be Burke because Danforth was the one who fixed their fake passports for them to get out of Port Said. Fabian rebuts, saying the passports were forged by a man called Danforth whom he has never seen and he is now convinced this man is Burke who probably intercepted the real Danforth on his way to Port Said.

Norvel is now scared and is not sure what to do about Danforth but

Fabian decides to honor Danforth's request to know their exact plans. For his part to get information from Madame Delacour about the specific day of the arrival of the French fleet, Norvel arranges to take Madame Delacour, Mary, and Rollo on a picnic out in the desert near the ancient tombs.

Burke again meets Mr. Moto at the antique shop and is clearly frustrated because he has never known so little at this stage of a case. Moto then tells Burke that he should leave now and they will meet again tomorrow. Just as they finish talking, there is a sudden knock on the shop's front door and Moto tells Burke to leave by the back door. At the shop's front door is Rollo who wants to buy an ancient scarab ring he sees in the window. Posing as Kuroki, Mr. Moto then sells Rollo the ring and claims it came from the tomb of Cleopatra.

After Rollo leaves the shop he is accosted by two muggers who knock him down and begin to rob him. Mr. Moto hears Rollo's cries for help and single-handedly fights off the two muggers. Patrons from Connie's Place, hearing there is a fight outside, also watch the fight and eagerly cheer the small-sized Kuroki on against the larger muggers.

Connie returns inside after the fight is over and tells Fabian and Hawkins that they just missed a good fight outside—"A little bit of a Japanese playing ping pong with a couple of bruisers." Fabian is stunned by Connie's description, which strongly reminds him of Mr. Moto—but Norvel had supposedly taken care of Moto. Connie also tells Fabian that the Japanese fellow is a man named Kuroki who owns the shop across the street and points him out as sitting at the next table. As Kuroki, Moto tells Fabian he has seen his funny act with the dummy and likes his act the best of all. Fabian is now very suspicious and tells Connie that he has a hunch that Kuroki may not be what he seems—but an impostor. Because he will be busy with Danforth the following day, he wants Connie to follow Kuroki as a precaution.

Early the next morning Fabian takes Burke, posing as Danforth, out to the *Vulcan* and explains that they do enough salvage work to satisfy both the port authorities *and* their investigators. Fabian also explains the sunken ship belongs to their employer who arranged to have it scuttled.

Eager to know more details, Burke presses further. Fabian reveals that divers are now planting explosives at the entrance to the Suez Canal and will eventually have the whole area mined with depth charges controlled from shore. After the first explosion, the leading ships of the fleet will be disabled and the entrance to the canal will be blocked.

For his plan to get rid of Burke, Fabian persuades Burke to observe things below in the diving bell alone. When Burke reaches the bottom, Fabian tells Burke through an intercom hookup that he knows who he really is and it's a shame they forgot to put oxygen tanks in the diving bell. Now hopeless, Burke tells Fabian he won't succeed but Fabian brags, "A thousand to one I do." Fabian then tells the crew to cut the cable. Moments later Burke dies of suffocation and the bubbles from the diving bell stop.

Meanwhile, Connie follows Mr. Moto to the office of the port commandant where Moto wants information about the *Vulcan*. The general (E.E. Clive) explains that the *Vulcan* is just a salvage ship working on a cargo boat wreck a couple of miles off shore in 15 fathoms of water. Moto is also told that the cargo boat got herself rammed and sunk a few weeks ago and the owners commissioned the *Vulcan* to salvage it.

When Fabian returns after killing Burke, Connie reports that she saw Kuroki go to the port commandant's office and came out 15 minutes later. All these coincidences cause Fabian to look again at Mr. Moto's page in his notebook that he crossed out earlier. Although there is no photograph of Moto, his written description does mention that Moto is short, a ju-jitsu expert, and is known to use doubles. Fabian is now convinced that Kuroki is indeed Mr. Moto and orders Capt. Hawkins to get rid of the Japanese agent.

Norvel then returns from his picnic and goes to the theater to tell Fabian that he was able to get Mary alone from her mother for a few moments and the little girl told him that she was going to see her father tomorrow morning. Fabian informs Norvel that the man listening in the next room at the theater was Kuroki, who is really Mr. Moto. Though Norvel can't believe it, Fabian is confident of his claim—"It fits too perfectly"—and tells Norvel that he ordered Hawkins to have Moto killed.

Connie also goes to the theater and heads to Fabian's room. From the outside she hears Fabian talking to Norvel, explaining the mines will blow up the flagship and during the commotion, no one will notice the *Vulcan* slip away. Fabian also mentions that all the papers and permits are in order and they even have visas for the "passengers." When Norvel opens the dressing room door to leave, Connie enters and Fabian admonishes her for coming backstage. However, she does likewise to him for lying to her that he was in the smuggling racket. In his defense, Fabian explains that he didn't want her to know what he really was up to but threatens her that she is now as much involved as he is.

Dressed as a beggar, Hakim easily sneaks into Kuroki's shop and conceals a time bomb in a cabinet located in the office. After reading a telegram, Moto checks his pocket watch and notices that the wall clock has stopped. At first he smiles, thinking nothing of the stopped clock. But then Moto hears a ticking noise which causes him to be very much concerned. He quickly looks around his office, locates the bomb, and throws it through a glass window after which it explodes.

Mr. Moto then goes outside and notices Hakim entering a warehouse on the wharf after giving a secret knock on the door. Just as Moto is about to go after Hakim, he bumps into Rollo who is walking around the wharf area as a tourist looking for adventure. Moto convinces Rollo that he is not Kuroki but is really Mr. Moto of the International Police. He appeals to Rollo's patriotism as an Englishman to quickly go to the port commandant to tell him that Moto needs his help. Moto then goes to the warehouse, gains entrance using the same knock, and subdues the thug inside the door with a karate chop to the neck.

Before Rollo can get to the authorities, he bumps into Norvel getting out of his cab. Rollo tells Norvel everything, not realizing that Norvel is part of the espionage ring, and that Mr. Moto has sent him to get the port commandant. Thinking quickly, Norvel suggests that his driver will go to the authorities instead and they should go back to the warehouse to assist Moto.

Now inside the warehouse, Novel tells Hawkins and Hakim that Moto is alive and Rollo now realizes that Novel is part of a gang. Mr. Moto comes out from his hiding place and takes on the saboteurs. Rollo is knocked out during the fighting and Hakim is able to hit Moto over the head with a chair which knocks the Japanese agent unconscious. When both regain consciousness, Moto and Rollo find themselves tied up and are about to be placed in sacks and thrown into the water. Moto sees a sharp piece of steel nearby and quietly grabs it, hoping to use it as a means to cut the ropes and free himself and Rollo.

Meanwhile, Norvel tells Fabian and Connie about Moto and the warehouse. They go to the warehouse and Fabian orders Norvel, Hakim, and Hawkins to throw the two sacks into the water. Disillusioned, Connie can't stand to be part of murdering the two men and runs back to her bar to call the port commandant for help. Fabian runs after her, stops her call, and strangles her until she falls unconscious to the floor but she is still alive. Fabian then returns to the warehouse to help Norvel with the final phase of their sabotage plot.

Once in the water, Moto uses the sharp metal to cut the ropes and the sacks to free both himself and Rollo and they rise to the water's surface. Once again Mr. Moto tells Rollo to go the port commandant and bring help.

On the wharf Fabian now sees the French fleet approaching the canal's entrance and has Norvel put on a diving suit. He tells Norvel that there is a detonator with a plunger below on the water's bottom and he will give three tugs on the air hose as his signal when to detonate the explosives. Moto overhears Fabian's instructions and dives below, knocking out Norvel, and prematurely sets off the explosives which causes the ships to safely change course.

Mr. Moto then surfaces again and on the wharf, struggles with Fabian. Connie then arrives and shoots Fabian, who falls mortally wounded into the water. Immediately thereafter, the British soldiers and Rollo arrive. Moto then tells the general that Connie had saved his life. On a hunch, Moto inspects the dummy and removes a piece of paper hidden inside Alf's head. The general also reads the paper but when Rollo asks the name of the country behind the plot, Moto responds through Alf, "Don't talk Mr. Moto, or you might lose your job!"

Commentary

Of all the films in the Mr. Moto series, *Mr. Moto's Last Warning* is the only one that is included in the book, *The Great Spy Pictures* and is one of only two *Mr. Moto* films listed in the book, *The Great Detective Pictures* (the other being *Mr. Moto in Danger Island*). Both books were co-written by James R. Parish and Michael R. Pitts. Listed in books with different genres, it seems to be a contradiction as *Mr. Moto's Last Warning* cannot be *both* a spy picture *and* a detective picture. Regardless, neither film is "great." As a spy picture, *Last Warning* covers the realm of international politics, a topic essentially avoided in the series' previous films. Despite being Japanese, Mr. Moto comes off well as a peacemaker between the major European powers.

Although the film is not the worst of the series, it does not rank near the top despite creditable performances by Ricardo Cortez, John Carradine, and Hollywood's professional cad, George Sanders. The film loses whatever momentum the previous entry, *Mysterious Mr. Moto*, would have provided it when *Last Warning* went into production. The impression is that the quality of the series is on the wane. The bumbling Englishman, Rollo Venables, adds very little to the plot other than providing Mr. Moto with an assistant. Spy adventures are normally filled with intrigue, action, mystery, and perhaps some romance, but they are not normally known for their comedic content.

There are several mysteries with this film starting with its title. There is no mention of any "warning" by Mr. Moto—first, last, or otherwise. The film probably would have better served if one of the film's working titles—*Mr. Moto in Egypt*—were used instead as the use of the exotic city of Port Said[39] does give the film an air of suspense and intrigue. Secondly, it is

---

39   Built in 1859, Port Said is an Egyptian city on the Mediterranean seacoast about 110 miles northeast of Cairo at the northern entrance to the Suez Canal. Port Said, named for Said Pasha, the khedive of Egypt at the time, is the administrative headquarters of the Suez Canal and its deepwater outer harbor is the principal fueling station for ships using the canal.

Clockwise from the upper left: Recardo Cortez, George Sanders, Teru Shimada, and John Carradine.

farfetched to conceive of the notion that if a French ship were blown up near the entrance to the Suez Canal, that the British would be the ones to be blamed for it. Despite all Mr. Moto's physical activity, he manages to keep his glasses on and in place, even when he is dumped into the water!

It is also hard to believe that for a shop that supposedly sells "valuable antiques," one can easily enter through an open window as Hakim does to plant a bomb. As if these items aren't already sufficient, it is also surprising that when Moto throws the bomb he discovers through a glass window, it doesn't explode when it breaks the glass, but explodes only when it hits the ground.

Perhaps the greatest mystery the film offers is the identity of the country that the sabotage ring works for and the viewers are left guessing. Richard Wires in his book, *John P. Marquand and Mr. Moto: Spy Adventures and Detective Films*, makes the case that the mystery country is Italy. In historical hindsight of the events leading up to World War II, it was fascist Italy, rather than Nazi Germany, who had long been engaged in a process of aggressive expansion in both the Mediterranean and the Middle East.

Fans of the *Mr. Moto* series were probably surprised to see someone other than Peter Lorre being called *Mr. Moto* near the beginning of the film. Viewers are already accustomed to seeing Moto in some form of disguise but this is the first and only film in which Mr. Moto uses a surrogate to assume his identity, if only for a while, while the real Mr. Moto impersonates a Oriental antique shop owner.

Film Notes

Production on *Mr. Moto's Last Warning* was from June 6 to June 29, 1938 under several working titles: *Mr. Moto No. 6*, *Mr. Moto in Egypt*, and *Winter Garden*. It was released almost seven months later on January 20, 1939 and is the only film of the *Mr. Moto* series in the public domain.

Interestingly enough, there are several, very quick references in this film to Charlie Chan—so quick, they might be considered subliminal. At the Sultana Theatre, there is a movie poster for *Charlie Chan in Honolulu* with a "Last Day" notice pasted over part of it. The theater's playbill also lists *Charlie Chan in Honolulu* starring Warner Oland as its first item. This film was the eighth *Charlie Chan* film in the popular series by Twentieth Century-Fox and was released one week prior to *Last Warning*. However, the actual *Honolulu* film featured Sidney Toler, *not* Warner Oland, in the title role of Charlie Chan. Although Oland was alive when *Last Warning* went into production, production of *Charlie Chan in Honolulu* started on October 31, 1938, almost three months after Oland died on August 6, 1938 of bronchial pneumonia. Some have thought that this mention of Oland was done a tribute to both Oland and the successful *Charlie Chan* series. (See the "Film Notes" section of *Mr. Moto's Gamble*.)

John Carradine appears in his second *Mr. Moto* film but it was Miles Mander who was originally cast for the role of Danforth. George Sanders, Hollywood's professional cad, really didn't want to be in this film, according to author Jon Tuska in his book, *The Detective in Hollywood*. Tuska recalls that Sanders took his displeasure out on director Norman Foster by running up huge restaurant bills and charged them to Foster's account. Nonetheless after filming the *Moto* entry, Sanders went on to star both as Simon Templar in the *Saint* and as Gay Lawrence in the *Falcon* detective film series, and he received an Oscar for the "Best Supporting Actor" category in *All About Eve* (1950). A young Teru Shimada, who appears as the substitute Mr. Moto, would eventually portray Mr. Osato in the James Bond thriller, *You Only Live Twice* (1967).

Peter Lorre as
Mr. MOTO in
DANGER ISLAND
HERSHOLT - DUFF
HYMER - - - LANE
AMES - DUMBRILLE
A 20th CENTURY FOX PICTURE

Mr. Moto in Danger Island (1939)

Twentieth Century-Fox Film Corp. Distributed by Twentieth Century-Fox Film Corp. Released: April 7, 1939; New York opening: week of March 20, 1939. Production: late November to late December 1938. Copyright Twentieth Century-Fox Film Corp., April 7, 1939; LP9023. Sound: Western Electric Mirrophonic Recording. B&W. 7 reels. 6,230 feet. 63 minutes. PCA certificate number 4939.

Director: Herbert I. Leeds. Associate producer: John Stone. Screen play: Peter Milne, based on story ideas by John Reinhardt and George Bricker from a novel [*Murder in Trinidad* (1933)] by John W. Vandercook. Based on the character "Mr. Moto" created by J. P. Marquand. Photography: Lucien Andriot, A.S.C. Art direction: Richard Day and Chester Gore. Set decorations: Thomas Little. Film editor: Harry Reynolds. Costumes: Herschel. Sound: Bernard Freericks and William H. Anderson. Musical direction: Samuel Kaylin. Assistant directors: Charles Hall* and Bill Forsyth.* Additional scenes: Jack Jungmeyer. Jr.* and Edith Skouras.* Continuity writers: John Reinhardt* and George Bricker.* Camera operator: Eddie Fitzgerald.* Assistant cameraman: Roger Sherman.* Head of camera department: Dan Clark.* Cutter: Harry Reynolds.* Set dresser: Walter Scott* and Al Orenbach.* Wardrobe man: Clinton Sandeen.* Recorder: W.P. Mathewson.* Boom man: Jim Burnett.* Hair stylist: Hazel Rogers.* Make up: Newton Jones.* Production manager: William Koenig.* Unit manger: Ben Wurtzell.* Script clerk: Helen Parker.* Grip: Hank Gersen.* Props: Don Greenwood.* Gaffer: Jack McAvoy.* Best boy: Ken McDonald.* Casting: Phillip Moore.* Cableman: Carl Daniels.* Still photographer: Anthony Ugrin.*

Source: Based on the character "Mr. Moto" created by J. P. Marquand

and the novel by John W. Vandercook [*Murder in Trinidad*, New York, 1933].

Cast

Peter Lorre *as* . . . . Mr. Moto [alias Shimura]
Jean Hersholt . . . . Sutter
Amanda Duff . . . . Joan Castle
Warren Hymer . . . . Twister McGurk
Richard Lane . . . . Commissioner Gordon
Leon Ames . . . . Commissioner Madero
Douglas Dumbrille . . . . [Commander] La Costa
Charles D. Brown . . . . Col. Thomas Castle
Paul Harvey . . . . Governor John Bentley
Robert Lowery . . . . Lieutenant George Bentley
Eddie Marr . . . . Captain Dahlen
Harry Woods . . . . Grant
Neely Edwards* . . . . Moore
Harry Strang* . . . . Henchman
George Magrill* . . . . Officer
Grace Hayle* . . . . Mrs. Brown
Tony Martelli,* Louis Mercier* . . . . Sergeants
Gloria Roy* . . . . Nurse
Edwin Stanley* . . . . Doctor
Jack Stoney,* Lee Shumway* . . . . Guards
Jimmie Dundee* . . . . Driver
Al Kikume* . . . . Sergeant
Ralph Dunn* . . . . Policeman
Lester Dorr* . . . . Ambulance attendant
Ray Walker* . . . . Ambulance attendant
Don Douglas* . . . . Police officer
Max Wagner* . . . . First member of crew
Oscar G. Hendrian* . . . . Second member of crew
Ward Bond* . . . . Sailor Sam
Juan Duval* . . . . Carlos
Renie Riano* . . . . Librarian
W R. Deming* . . . . Drunk

Edward Keane* . . . . Washington official
Willie Best* . . . . Boat pilot

————————————

*Uncredited

"One cannot gain the confidence of criminals, unless one is branded a criminal."

—Mr. Moto to Twister McGuirk

The Story

Mr. Moto is aboard the *San Juan*, a ship bound for Puerto Rico from New Orleans, and is at ringside watching a wrestling match between Twister McGuirk (Warren Hymer) and Sailor Sam (Ward Bond). Watching with him is Joan Castle (Amanda Duff), an attractive college co-ed who is going home during a college break to see both her father, who is the police chief there, and her fiancé. When Sailor Sam appears about to injure Twister, Joan is horrified but Mr. Moto assures her that it isn't as terrible as it looks—"You see, the art of professional wrestling consists of three parts brawn, two parts acting, and but one little part of skill."

Sailor Sam is distracted when overhears Mr. Moto's explanation of the sport to Joan. This then allows Twister McGuirk to pin him and win the match. Irate about Moto having causing him to lose, Sailor Sam reaches over the ring's top rope and pulls Moto up by the collar with one hand saying, "You little beetle! It's your fault I lost this match." He then yanks Moto into the ring and promises to show him a lesson in what real wrestling is. But it is Moto who gives the lesson—using ju-jitsu to easily overcome the much larger opponent—all to the delight of the sailors in the audience.

Twister congratulates Mr. Moto saying, "I've seen everything. A little shrimp like you throwing a sailor. It gets me." Twister also worries that if Moto was a professional wrestler, he could never get to be world's champion. However Moto assures the brawny wrestler that he can depend on him to remain an amateur. Mr. Moto then graciously accepts McGuirk's request to demonstrate some of his ju-jitsu throws. Just before he attempts an encore, Moto grabs his side, grimacing in pain, and thinking that he must have strained some muscles there. Twister quickly picks up Mr. Moto and carries him to the ship's medical facility.

Meanwhile in the office the Governor of Puerto Rico, Gov. John Bentley (Paul Harvey) is telling some of his political associates and subordinates that he is tired of excuses about their inability to stop the smuggling of cheap diamonds from South America through Puerto Rico, thereby glutting the world market. Bentley is also concerned that diamond values will collapse if the smuggling is allowed to continue unchecked. At this gathering are Commissioner Gordon (Richard Lane), Commissioner Madero (Leon Ames), chief of police Col. Castle (Charles D. Brown), the governor's nephew Lt. George Bentley (Robert Lowery), and Mr. Sutter (Jean Hersholt), a local shipper whose ships are thought to have been used by the smugglers.

If the smuggling wasn't enough, the governor reminds everyone that Rodney Graham, a special investigator sent from Washington was murdered in Puerto Rico. Looking at Col. Castle, Bentley complains that weeks have gone by and still no arrests have been made. He also lets it be known that the diamond syndicate is putting pressure on him. Backbiting then breaks out among the individuals but soon stops after the governor tells them that their feuding won't solve anything.

Bentley tries to soothe Col. Castle's feelings, encouraging him to take a long rest, which Castle claims is the same thing as asking him to resign. Castle refuses to resign and to "leave the desks clear for Mr. Moto." Everyone is surprised to hear the mention of Mr. Moto's name. Gov. Bentley asks Col. Castle how he knows Mr. Moto is coming to investigate and Castle responds that it is his business to know things. The governor tells everyone that Moto's coming wasn't his idea—Mr. Moto has been retained by the diamond syndicate.

Suddenly, the governor is handed a radiogram sent from Joan Castle. He tells everyone that Mr. Moto, traveling on the *San Juan*, has just come down with appendicitis and orders Commissioner Gordon to have an ambulance ready at the dock the next day to take Moto to the hospital for an emergency operation.

When the *San Juan* docks, George Bentley (Joan Castle's fiancé), the governor, her father the police chief, and Commissioner Gordon are all there to meet Joan. Gordon is the last of the group to welcome her home saying, "This island is no jewel without you, no matter what the travel literature says."

Mr. Moto is then brought ashore, carried on stretcher covered by a blanket. Moto greets the governor, "I regret that I have to make my entrance into your beautiful country, like a poor fish, packed in ice." Moto is then placed in the waiting ambulance along with Twister, who insists that he come along.

The ambulance departs and moments later two ambulance attendants arrive at the pier in a cab to warn Commissioner Gordon that two people hijacked their ambulance and has kidnapped Moto. Inevitably, the stolen ambulance pulls into a clandestine warehouse where Capt. Dahlen (Eddie Marr), a small-time boat skipper and a member of the smuggling ring, knows about Moto's appendicitis and wants Moto to tell him what information Graham sent to Washington. Despite being threatened with a gun, Moto bravely responds that the information is confidential and he is left with two fatal choices—to die from either appendicitis or a bullet.

Before Dahlen can do anything, Mr. Moto fires a gun from underneath his blanket at Dahlen and with Twister McGuirk's assistance, both tangle with the many gang members. A few moments later the police and the governor arrive but most of the gang escape to a nearby river where they have a boat waiting. Gov. Bentley apologizes to Mr. Moto for taking so long to find the warehouse but they were given the slip—not knowing where Moto was until they heard the shooting. Nonetheless, the governor is puzzled as to how the kidnappers knew that the Japanese agent had appendicitis. Moto sees some mud on the warehouse floor, which he thinks might be a clue as to the location of the gang's hideout.

McGuirk returns to the warehouse after having unsuccessfully chased some of the gang members. Because Mr. Moto is now standing talking with the governor, he asks Moto if his appendix is OK. Moto matter-of-factly replies, "Oh, that useless member of my anatomy was removed ten years ago." After pausing for a moment, McGuirk then realizes that is friend's appendicitis attack was a trick and Moto must be on a case. He also wants to tag along and help.

The governor expresses his disappointment that Mr. Moto's scheme to trap the smugglers wasn't successful, but Moto disagrees. As he had suspected, the events prove that there is an information leak in the governor's office and that the kidnappers are only carrying out orders of their leader. Even though Gov. Bentley assures Mr. Moto that, according to their plan, he made it known to those in his office that Moto had appendicitis, the governor vouches that those present are honest men and it is farfetched that any of them could be involved. Nonetheless, Mr. Moto tells the governor that he would soon like to question the so-called "honest" men.

In Gov. Bentley's office, Moto meets with all those involved—Sutter, Commissioners Gordon and Madero, George Bentley, and Col. Castle. He

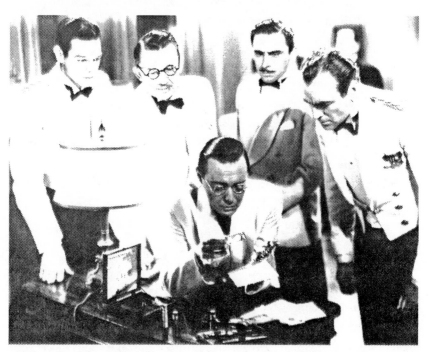

Peter Lorre looks for fingerprints on a dagger as Robert Lowery, Jean Hersholt, Leon Ames, and Richard Lane look on.

expresses his disappointment that one of them betrayed him because only they knew of his alleged appendicitis. However his questioning yields very little to go on. Moto then discovers that a man named La Costa (Douglas Dumbrille) is using the office intercom to quietly listen in on their conversation in the governor's office. When confronted and accused by Sutter of intentionally activating the intercom, La Costa warns Sutter that he himself has yet to explain how he was the first person to discover Graham's body with a knife plunged through the heart.

Before dismissing everyone, Bentley invites all present to a small welcome home party he and his nephew George are hosting for Miss Castle. Once everyone leaves, Gov. Bentley shows Moto some items found at the dead agent's apartment, among which is a San Juan public library card. At the library Mr. Moto is told that Graham had signed out four books which, the librarian (Renie Riano) complains, have yet to be returned. In particular was a book about Black Tarrant, a pirate who lived about three hundred years ago and whose hideout was the swamps of Point Salinas—a reputed haunting ground for ghosts. In the library stacks nearby is Sutter, who is pretending to be browsing through a book but is actively listening to Moto's conversation with the librarian.

Acting on a hunch from clues of the library book titles, Mr. Moto charters a small boat to investigate the swamps around Point Salinas. The boat pilot (Willie Best), when told of their intended destination, becomes frightened because local superstition holds the area is haunted with ghosts. Twister dismisses the pilot's fears as silly but the pilot insists—"Many people goes into the swamps and nobody ever sees 'em alive again." Once they reach the shore, Mr. Moto uses an oar to collect a quantity of swamp mud. Then a rifle shot is fired at Twister from someone hiding in the bushes just as they are about to leave.

Safely back now in his hotel room, Mr. Moto examines the mud both from the swamp and which was left on the floor from the shoes of the kidnappers at the warehouse. Under a strong magnifying glass, both Moto and Twister conclude that the mud samples bear the same characteristics and that the kidnappers came from the swamp. Moto also deduces that Graham was murdered because he too was attracted to the swamp as the possible hideout of the diamond smugglers.

Twister has an electric shaver, but when he plugs it into the electric socket in the bathroom, nothing happens. As the same time, a hotel attendant brings freshly pressed tuxedos for Moto and McGuirk to wear at the party that evening. After laying the clothes out on the bed, the attendant asks Mr. Moto if he wants him to draw his bath, to which Moto says *yes*. Moments later they hear the man fall to the floor. Moto investigates and finds that the poor fellow was electrocuted—the bathtub was wired to the electrical socket and was the reason Twister's shaver didn't work earlier.

Meanwhile at Col. Castle's residence, daughter Joan is laying out her father's clothes for the party. When she opens a dresser drawer, Joan finds a box which contains a number of large diamonds. Her father then arrives home and tells her that he won't be going to her party, giving the excuse that he is tired and the diamond smuggling case has been hard on him. He confesses to Joan that he is of the opinion that Bentley and the others think that he is mixed up with the smuggling and they want him to resign, but he refuses to. Despite her urgings, her father still refuses to go to the party.

Once at the party, Joan asks George why he and his uncle want her father to resign. Shocked that she would ask such a question, George tells his fiancée that they do not want her father to resign and they are genuinely concerned for his health—Col. Castle had been worrying himself to pieces about the diamond smuggling case. The nephew further assures Joan that neither he nor his uncle consider her father to be involved with the smuggling.

Also at the party, Mr. Moto is seen attracted to a cabinet containing ancient artifacts from the island's past, most of which as the governor proudly points out, once belonged to the island's premier pirate. "Black Tarrant," Moto correctly adds. Commissioner Madero then mentions that the pirate was always able to escape and the authorities were never able to find his hiding place. Moto again retorts, "You mean the great Salinas swamp?" Moto's authoritative knowledge of the island's geography and history both surprises and impresses the governor and Madero, the latter who cautions Moto not to go near the swamp as the local natives believe it to be haunted with the ghost of Black Tarrant.

Mr. Moto then eyes an old map of the swamp in the cabinet and examines it. Sutter then confesses to Moto that just before Graham was killed, the investigator thought there was a connection between the swamp and the smuggling. Mr. Moto tells Sutter that he saw him at the library earlier but Sutter explains that he often goes there. Moto then politely bows and thanks Sutter for the information. Nonetheless, Moto has a cautious look as Sutter leaves.

The governor receives a call from Col. Castle who has an important matter he wishes to discuss privately and he will be coming over immediately. In front of several people, the governor tells Castle that he will meet him in his upstairs bedroom.

Joan Castle decides to telephone her father, unaware that he is now coming over to see the governor. When she picks up one of the hallway telephones, she hears Capt. Dahlen talking to an unknown person at the party about a new shipment of diamonds that are to be loaded aboard a boat that evening. Unfortunately, George startles her, causing Joan to drop

the handset. She is now unable to hear any more of the conversation because the line is now disconnected.

Joan and George hurry to the governor's room to notify him of this new information. Meanwhile through, Twister McGuirk is roaming around the upstairs hallway trying to find Madero, of whom he has been suspicious for some time. When he opens the door to the governor's room, McGuirk sees Col. Castle kneeling over the governor's dead body. Joan and George arrive moments later and when her father stands up, he appears to be dazed and holding his head as if he had been struck unconscious from behind.

Mr. Moto also arrives on the scene and examines the murder weapon—a knife which had been taken from a display collection on the wall in the governor's office. He notices it to be similar to the knife used to kill Graham and the only fingerprints found on the knife are those of the police chief who has admitted that he had touched the knife when he found the body. Castle also confesses about the purpose of his visit—to resign now because he didn't want to wait until tomorrow. Commissioner Gordon now wants to place Castle under arrest but Mr. Moto persuades Gordon to let Castle go home on his own recognizance.

Now at home, the accused police chief has been sedated and is sleeping quietly. Joan confides in Mr. Sutter and George Bentley that she found some diamonds hidden in her father's bedroom.

Joan also mentions the telephone conversation she overheard about a new shipment of diamonds but she couldn't recognize the voice. Afraid, Joan says she didn't know what to do because Commissioner Gordon already suspects her father of being involved and would have thought her father was on the telephone. Sutter says he will take care of the diamonds and tells Joan not to worry, and to stay close to her father until she hears from him.

George Bentley tells Gordon and Moto about the telephone conversation Joan overheard. Gordon is now convinced that Col. Castle is guilty, figuring that Gov. Bentley heard Castle talking and Castle had to kill him. Sutter then suggests the possibility that someone could have planted the diamonds in Castle's house. Nonetheless, Gordon says he is going to have

Col. Castle arrested but Moto recommends that it would be wiser if Gordon questions Col. Castle quietly before making any arrest that could cause a scandal. Gordon reluctantly agrees.

The next morning Gordon, Sutter, George Bentley, Twister, and Moto go to Col. Castle's house but find no one home. Gordon then feels tricked and says he should have arrested Castle last night. He calls police headquarters and orders an all points bulletin to arrest the missing police chief on the charge of murder.

Suddenly the governor's aide comes in and hands Commissioner Gordon a cablegram. After reading its contents, Gordon orders the police to arrest Mr. Moto and his accomplice, Twister McGuirk. The cablegram Gordon received was sent from New York to Gov. Bentley—"Have just learned that notorious criminal, Shimura, in Puerto Rico posing as me. Hold him until my arrival. Will be on tomorrow's plane. Moto." Gordon confesses he was suspicious of the small Japanese from the start but before the police can take Moto and Twister away, the pair overpower their guards and escape.

Now on the run, hiding, and believing he has been unfairly accused, McGuirk strongly protests to Mr. Moto for getting him into trouble. Moto then confesses that he himself sent that cablegram as a trick. When Twister asks why, Moto replies, "One cannot gain the confidence of criminals, unless one is branded a criminal."

That evening, Moto and Twister return to the Salinas swamp where they wait to be captured by the smugglers. Once they are apprehended, Moto asks they be taken to whomever is currently in charge. When they meet a man named Grant (Harry Woods), they also encounter Joan and her father being held by the smugglers who promised they would protect her father until he was proven innocent. Joan sees Mr. Moto and pleads to Grant that Moto is a detective who wants to convict her father. However Moto refutes her claims and says it was all an impersonation. One of the smugglers even shows Joan a newspaper naming the Japanese as Shimura.

Grant is not sure what to believe but decides to hold Moto and Twister captive until Dahlen returns. However the pair soon overpower their guard, escape, and proceed to investigate the smuggler's camp. In time

Moto finds that diamonds are being smuggled inside of coconuts and he is satisfied he now has enough evidence to clear the accused chief of police. Mr. Moto and Twister sneak back to their boat and head back to San Juan.

While temporarily taking over the duties of the slain governor, Commissioner Gordon receives a telephone call from Washington. Now impatient, Gordon inquires of the caller where Moto is because he wasn't on the plane as he said he would be in the cablegram. The caller (Edward Keane) insists that Moto has already been in Puerto Rico for a week but Gordon says he received a message saying the man claiming to be Mr. Moto was a dangerous criminal named Shimura who escaped before he could put in jail.

When asked to describe this man, Gordon describes the man. "He's short, round face, not much over five feet tall, big eyes, always wears glasses." The caller assures Gordon that this man *is* Moto. His turning fugitive is just one of his tricks and recalls that Moto once even pretended to have escaped from Devil's Island. When Mr. Moto and McGuirk finally show up at Gordon's office, they are first captured by the police, but the embarrassed commissioner orders the police to release the pair because the man is really Mr. Moto.

Mr. Moto and Twister, now accompanied by Sutter and the police, return by boat to the smugglers' swamp hideout. As they arrive, they see Dahlen speeding away in his boat which has Joan and her father locked in the cabin below. As they gather speed and close in, Dahlen turns and fires his gun which prompts the police to respond in kind. Moto then tells the police to stop their shooting as he wants to capture Dahlen alive. However, Dahlen continues to shoot and wounds Sutter in the hand. Despite Moto's admonition, Sutter shoots Dahlen in the back, causing the boat to spin out of control. The police boat eventually pulls along side and Moto jumps onto the fleeing boat and rescues Col. Castle and Joan. Rushing to Dahlen's body to feel his pulse, Mr. Moto tells Sutter that Dahlen is not dead, and requests Dahlen be immediately taken to the hospital.

At the hospital the attending doctor (Edwin Stanley) tells Mr. Moto and the others that Dahlen is resting quietly and he refuses to allow anyone to question the wounded skipper until he regains some of his strength. Mr.

Moto then inquires if eight o'clock that evening will be sufficient time for questioning. The doctor agrees and Moto requests everyone return to the hospital at eight.

That night at the hospital just before eight o'clock, Sutter arrives but goes around to a side window. Climbing up to the window of Dahlen's room, Sutter throws a knife at the sleeping Dahlen. He then jumps down to the ground but Mr. Moto, who had anticipated such an attempt on Dahlen's life, is waiting. Moto jumps on top of Sutter and quickly apprehends him.

Inside the hospital Mr. Moto unmasks Sutter as the one who murdered Dahlen—to prevent him from exposing Sutter as the real head of the smuggling ring. "Your aim with the knife was true for the third time, Mr. Sutter," Moto commends. Commissioner Gordon then realizes that Sutter also murdered Graham and Gov. Bentley.

Mr. Moto proceeds to explain that Graham was killed because his scrutiny was leading him to the Salinas swamp. When Col. Castle started his investigation, Sutter pretended to help his friend but knew in advance every move the police were taking and also knew of Moto's arrival with appendicitis. Mr. Moto further points out that when he was not killed in the warehouse, Sutter later booby-trapped his bathtub, killing the hotel attendant instead. Dahlen was careless to telephone Sutter at the governor's party to inform him of Moto's escape and when Sutter was surprised by the governor, Sutter killed him.

Sutter counters, "A fine string of guesses Mr. Moto, but you can't prove one of them." However Moto begs to differ. He calmly mentions Sutter proved all the guesses when he threw the knife into Dahlen, who would have talked if captured and that Sutter shot Dahlen against his explicit orders not to.

George Bentley then criticizes Mr. Moto for allowing Sutter to kill a helpless man, to which Moto reveals that Dahlen was already dead when he earlier reached his body in the boat—"You really shouldn't have killed him *twice*, Mr. Sutter." Again embarrassed but relieved, Commissioner Gordon tells Moto that he has a lot to apologize for and congratulates Moto.

Commentary

As mentioned previously, *Mr. Moto in Danger Island* is included in the book, *The Great Detective Pictures*, co-written by James R. Parish and Michael R. Pitts. To say this film is "great," as the book's title would suggest, is a gross overstatement. The film is considered by most to be the weakest of the eight *Mr. Moto* films with Peter Lorre in the title role. It also should be noted that this is one of two films of the Lorre series that Norman Foster was not associated with, either as its director or its scenarist. His absence is evident despite performances by capable actors such as Jean Hersholt, Douglas Dumbrille, Leon Ames, and Robert Lowery. As the last film in production, the decline in the quality of the series was already evident.

One problem any fan of the *Mr. Moto* series has in this film is trying to figure out why the U.S. government would send a *Japanese* agent to Puerto Rico to investigate the smuggling of diamonds. Of course this connection would be somewhat plausible if Mr. Moto is identified as working for the International Police. However, no such connection is never mentioned or implied in this film.

Warren Hymer, who portrays the intellectually challenged wrestler Twister McGurk, mangles the English language with his malapropisms in much the same way Leo Gorcey did in his role as Terence Aloysious "Slip" Mahoney in *The Bowery Boys* film series. Charles Mitchell, in his review of the *Mr. Moto* series in a *Classic Images* article, remarks that "His [Hymer's] stock character is so broad and contrived that it ruins every scene he is in." In addition, Willie Best has a small part where he is cast in the stereotyped role of the Negro who is frightened of ghosts and his own shadow.

The film is supposed to be a whodunit, and despite the large collection of red herrings, it's not too difficult for the viewers to see the accumulation of clues that all point to Sutter as both the murderer and the leader of the diamond smuggling ring. He is the first on the scene when Rodney Graham, the previous investigator, is murdered. His ships are suspected of being used by the diamond smugglers. Commander La Costa accuses Sutter of charging exorbitant shipping prices for his crops. As the owner of the shipping line and having access to the names of the passengers sailing on the *San Juan*, Sutter is already aware of Mr. Moto's planned arrival in Puerto Rico. And finally, Mr. Moto notices Sutter lurking in a nearby aisle when Moto visits the San Juan Public Library. Being friends with the police chief and the island's governor,[40] Sutter is then privy to all the necessary facts and is always one step ahead of the law.

Film Notes

Mr. Moto in Danger Island was the eighth and last film of the series to be produced with Peter Lorre in the title role. When it was released on April 7, 1939 however, it was the seventh film in the series—released three months before *Mr. Moto Takes a Vacation*. While in production, the working film titles were: *Mr. Moto in Puerto Rico* and *Mr. Moto in Trinidad*.

The film was originally intended to be a 1938 *Charlie Chan* picture, *Charlie Chan in Trinidad*, which was based on an original screenplay by John Reinhardt and adapted from the 1933 novel, *Murder in Trinidad*, by John W. Vandercook. When Warner Oland died in August 1938, the *Charlie Chan in Trinidad* screenplay was transformed by George Bricker one month later as *Mr. Moto in Trinidad*. Peter Milne changed the setting from Trinidad to Puerto Rico and some other story details. The film was then released as *Mr. Moto in Danger Island*.

While on the connection to other films, it is revealed in *Mr. Moto in Danger Island* that Mr. Moto once pretended to have escaped from Devil's Island. Fans of the series will easily recall Mr. Moto posing as the murderer Ito Matsuka and is seen escaping from Devil's Island at the beginning of the film, *Mysterious Mr. Moto* (1938).

It is indeed ironic that the role of the murderer is played by Jean

---

40   As *Danger Island* was made in 1938, the actual governor of Puerto Rico was Blanton Winship, who was appointed in 1933 by President Roosevelt, but was summarily removed by FDR on May 12, 1939 for his many acts of misfeasance and nonfeasance. Admiral William Daniel Leahy succeeded Winship as Governor of Puerto Rico until 1941.

Hersholt (also the uncle of actor Leslie Nielsen), who in real life was well-known for his philanthropic activities. One of these helped build the Motion Picture Country Home and Hospital in Woodland Hills, California. He was honored with special Oscars in 1939 and 1941 and the Academy of Motion Picture Arts and Sciences established a humanitarian award in his honor. Following his role in the *Mr. Moto* film, Hersholt went on to star as the folksy Dr. Paul Christian in six films. Richard Lane went on to play Inspector Farraday 14 times in the *Boston Blackie* film series between 1941 and 1949.

One interesting bit of trivia that probably goes unnoticed by most viewers of the film is that when McGurk asks Moto if his appendix is OK, Moto replies, "Oh, that useless member of my anatomy was removed ten years ago." Well, Peter Lorre actually *did* have his appendix removed about ten years earlier than the filming of *Danger Island*. During his early years in the theater in the late 1920s, Lorre developed appendicitis and his father arranged for the appendectomy to be performed in Zurich. Postoperative complications required that his gall bladder be also removed.

Mr. Moto Takes a Vacation (1939)

Twentieth Century-Fox Film Corp. Distributed by Twentieth Century-Fox Film Corp. Released: July 7, 1939; New York opening: week of June 19, 1939. Production: late August to late September 1938. Copyright Twentieth Century-Fox Film Corp., July 7, 1939; LP8966. Sound: Western Electric Mirrophonic Recording. B&W. 6 reels. 5,632 feet. 65 minutes. PCA cert no. 4649.

Director: Norman Foster. Original screenplay: Philip MacDonald and Norman Foster, based on the character "Mr. Moto" created by John P. Marquand. Photography: Charles Clarke, A.S.C. Art direction: Bernard Herzbrun and Haldane Douglas. Set decorations: Thomas Little. Film editor: Norman Colbert. Costumes: Herschel. Sound: Alfred Bruzlin and William H. Anderson. Musical direction: Samuel Kaylin. Producer: Sol M Wurtzel.* Assistant directors: Jasper Blystone* and David Hall.* Production manager: V. L. McFadden*

Cast

Peter Lorre *as* . . . . Mr. Moto [alias Professor Heinrich
. . . . von Kleinroth *and* Mr. Shimako]
Joseph Schildkraut . . . . Hendrik Manderson [alias for Metaxa]
Lionel Atwill . . . . Professor Hildebrand
Virginia Field . . . . Eleanor Kirke
John King . . . . Howard Stevens
Iva Stewart . . . . Susan French
George P. Huntley, Jr. . . . . Archie Featherstone
Victor Varconi . . . . Paul Borodoff
John Bleifer. . . . . Wendling
Honorable Wu . . . . Wong

Morgan Wallace . . . . David Perez [alias Dr. Pascal]
Anthony Warde . . . . Joe Rubla
Harry Strang . . . . O'Hara
John Davidson . . . . Prince Suleid
Willie Best* . . . . Driver
Stanley Blystone* . . . . Ship's officer
Robert Winckler* . . . . Boy
Tom O'Grady,* Isabel La Mal* . . . . Ship passengers
Bobby Hale* . . . . Steward
Leyland Hodgson* . . . . Waiter on ship
George Chandler* . . . . Press cameraman at museum
Ralph Dunn,* Lee Phelps,* Pat O'Malley*. . . . . Policemen
William Gould* . . . . Police captain
Chick Collins* . . . . Driver of armored car
Lester Dorr*. . . . . Reporter
Jack Clifford*. . . . . Sergeant on motorcycle
Brooks Benedict* . . . . Gangster
Jimmy Aubrey* . . . . Drunk panhandler
Victor Wong* . . . . Restaurant proprietor
Chan Suey*. . . . . Musician
Mae Leung* . . . . Chinese singer
Jadine Wong* . . . . Dancer
Iris Wong* . . . . Waitress
Sam Hayes* . . . . Radio announcer
Major Sam Harris* . . . . Professor
Eddie Abdo* . . . . Arabian officer
Hank Mann* . . . . unnamed

_____

*Unbilled

"Uneasy lies the hand that bears the crown."

—Mr. Moto to Prince Suleid

The Story

Well-known archaeologist Howard Stevens (John King) of the San Francisco Museum is in the Arabian desert searching for the lost crown of the Queen of Sheba. With him is Professor Heinrich von Kleinroth of Vienna, who is Mr. Moto in disguise. Kleinroth enthusiastically proclaims that the object just found bears the emblem of the Lion of Judea—the Seal of Solomon.[41] Stevens agrees and he is now holding in his hand the crown of *Balkis*—the Queen of Sheba,[42] which has been missing for 3,000 years.

In his tent with Prince Suleid (John Davidson), Stevens is cautioned by the Viennese archaeologist that he must now be careful to guard his new-found treasure, which Prince Suleid adds, exceeds the wealth of the Aga Khan.[43] When Stevens leaves to talk to waiting journalists about the his dis-

---

41   Actually the Seal of Solomon is now known as the "Star of David," or *Magen David* in Hebrew—a six-pointed star. On the other hand, the "Lion of Judea" is an often used symbol motif showing a lion, and is the central design of the seal for the modern city of Jerusalem.

42   The Queen of Sheba (known to Arabs as *Bilqis* or *Balkis*) visited Solomon after hearing about the fame of his wisdom. According to legend, Solomon and the Queen of Sheba married and they had a son, Menelik, from which the Ethiopian royal line claimed descent. Sheba is the biblical name of a region, also known as Saba, of southern Arabia, including present-day Yemen and the Hadhramaut.

The Queen of Sheba is mentioned prominently in the respective holy books revered by Christians, Jews, and Muslims. The Bible mentions the meeting with King Solomon of Israel (thought to have occurred around 950–930 B.C.) where the Queen made the journey north to Solomon's courts "to test him with hard questions" (II Chronicles 9). The Qur'an also refers to the Queen's meeting with Solomon (Sura XXVII—*Al-Naml*, The Ant), but tells of the king traveling south to meet at her capital, Marib. Jesus praises the Queen of the South—Semitic for "Yemen"—as a righteous woman for seeking King Solomon's wisdom (Matthew 12:42). Ethiopian folklore claims that the queen returned from Jerusalem carrying Solomon's child (Menelik).

43   The Aga Kahn is the title of the religious leader and imam of the Ismaili Nizari sect of Islam.

covery, Mr. Moto tells Prince Suleid, who knows of Moto's impersonation and whose men are assigned to guard the crown until it is on the boat to San Francisco, that he believes that a thief will eventually make an attempt to steal the crown. Prince Suleid agrees, feeling that a valuable object like the crown will attract many thieves, but Mr. Moto believes that a certain thief will be compelled to try. Moto explains further that this person suffers from a psychopathic disorder—"The more unobtainable the object, the more determined he grows to possess it."

To support his deduction, Mr. Moto brings to mind the daring theft of some jewels from the Tower of London some time ago. Suleid says that a man named Metaxa, who no one has ever seen, was suspected of the theft but adds that Metaxa has been reported to be dead for several years. Moto however disagrees and points to several high-profile thefts in the past few years that have remained unsolved and that the *modus operandi* is characteristic of Metaxa.

Leaving Arabia, Stevens takes the crown aboard a ship on its voyage to the waiting museum in San Francisco. Mr. Moto is also aboard, no longer disguised as Prof. Kleinroth, but is now traveling *incognito* as a Japanese tourist named Mr. Shimako. Also making the trip is Howard Stevens and an attractive woman, Eleanor Kirke (Virginia Field), who seems to have more than a passing interest concerning the crown.

Unfortunately Mr. Moto's cover is blown when Archie Featherstone (George P. Huntley, Jr.), a bumbling British tourist and amateur detective who is an acquaintance of Mr. Moto, bumps into the Japanese and instinctively blurts out, "I say Mr. Moto, how marvelous to meet *you* like this!" in front of Eleanor and Stevens who are surprised to learn Shimako's true identity. Stevens then asks Mr. Moto if he is on a case and why he is hiding his identity. The Japanese agent responds the he is on vacation and was simply avoiding any possibility of business.

The entire incident is overheard by Wendling (John Bleifer), a confederate of Joe Rubla (Anthony Warde), who along with David Perez (Morgan Wallace), a jeweler in San Francisco's Chinatown, are planing to steal the crown. Wendling sends Perez a radiogram from the ship that Rubla's "friend" Mr. Moto is on board the same ship with the crown. If not to guard the crown, Perez now worries why Moto is on the ship, but Rubla counters, "So what? You think a little Japanese dick is going to scare me?" Perez however knows Moto's reputation and is scared of him—wanting no part of the operation until Rubla agrees to rub out Moto.

While sitting at a table at a party celebrating the ship's last night at sea prior to their arrival in port the following day, Featherstone reminds Mr. Moto of his uncle, Sir Hector, who is at Scotland Yard. Featherstone tells Moto that his uncle thinks that a super criminal named Metaxa, officially listed as dead, is still alive and quietly hiding in America. Moto is glad to hear that someone has the same suspicion he does.

When the ship docks in San Francisco, Stevens is met by Hendrik Manderson (Joseph Schildkraut), a crotchety old philanthropist who walks with a cane and who helped finance the expedition. Also on hand is Fremont museum curator Professor Hildebrand (Lionel Atwill), and his secretary, Susan French (Iva Stewart), who is strongly attracted to Stevens.

At the pier, Mr. Moto takes a cab and is secretly followed in another

Peter Lorre goes over museum security with Joseph Schildkraut and Lionel Atwill.

cab by Wendling, who Rubla now orders to kill Moto. Also at the pier is an armored car and motorcycle escort waiting to take the jeweled crown to the Fremont Museum, but something doesn't seem right as Joe Rubla is seen disguised as an armored car guard. Moments after the armored car leaves, two policemen arrive and tell the police chief (William Gould) that the armored car was stolen and the guards are phonies.

Featherstone then commands a car driven by a driver (Willie Best) with dubious driving skills. The two pursue Rubla and his gang to a narrow side street where the thieves proceed to unload the stolen items. Featherstone remains to watch the thieves while his driver is told to summon the police. Moments later the police arrive and after a brief exchange of gunfire, they retrieve the stolen items and capture all the criminals except for Rubla who escapes. Featherstone brags to the police chief that he got a good look at the ring leader and can easily identify him.

Back at David Perez's apartment above his jewelry store, Rubla realizes that he is now a wanted man and boasts to the jeweler that he'll take care of "that Limey" just as he took care of Mr. Moto. But Wendling returns and gives Rubla the bad news that he didn't have a chance to kill Moto as he had planned. He followed Moto to the city hall but the Japanese went out to lunch with the chief of police.

Now a tourist, Mr. Moto visits Chinatown that evening and as luck would have it, he unexpectedly meets Archie Featherstone right in front of Perez's jewelry shop. Inside the shop unknown to Mr. Moto and Featherstone, Rubla and Perez observe the pair though the shop window. Having failed in a previous attempt to kill Moto, Rubla now wants to shoot Moto through the window but Perez convinces the gangster that it would not be a good idea.

Because Archie claims he now can identify the men who stole the armored car, Moto cautions him that the thieves now undoubtedly would want to kill him. Moto then offers Featherstone some tongue-in-cheek advice—"If you really wish to be a successful detective, there's one golden rule you must follow . . . Never become a fatality."

Suddenly a gun shot just misses Mr. Moto and hits the jewelry shop window. Moto quickly deduces the bullet came from across the street rather than from inside the shop. Looking across the street, Moto sees a shadowy figure running away. Seeing the gunman's phenomenal agility that allows him to escape now convinces Moto that Archie Featherstone's Uncle Hector's hunch is correct—Metaxa is alive and is in San Francisco. Moto also concludes that none of the men who earlier tried to steal the crown at the pier could be Metaxa as the methods are far too different.

The next day, the Fremont Museum is holding its unveiling of the crown in a specially prepared exhibit room with an elaborate alarm system that includes invisible light beams. David Perez, using the alias of Dr. Pascal, gains admission to the exhibit along with Paul Borodoff (Victor Varconi), a bogus insurance investigator and an accomplice of Eleanor Kirke who also have plans to steal the ancient crown.

While Prof. Hildebrand goes to great lengths to explain the elaborate alarm system the museum installed for the exhibit to the invited guests, Perez is covertly making a small sketch of the floor plan and security details of the exhibit room. Hildebrand then attempts to demonstrate the alarm system but it fails to operate. Embarrassed, Hildebrand nonetheless opens the exhibit to the guests and requests that he, Moto, and Manderson proceed to his office where the alarm's controls are hidden. There, Hildebrand finds that the alarm was turned off earlier by Howard Stevens without his knowledge. Just before Hildebrand is to throw the switch to reactivate the alarm, he is stopped by Mr. Moto. Manderson then chides Hildebrand that he has probably obliterated any fingerprints that may have been on the switch. Disheartened, the curator explains, "Oh dear, what a big *zany* I am!" to which Manderson happily agrees. Under questioning, Mr. Moto learns that only Prof. Hildebrand, Manderson, Howard Stevens, and the installers knew the location of the hidden alarm switch.

In the exhibit area just before the exhibit is about to close for the day, Archie Featherstone is admiring the crown of Sheba and is standing next to Perez masquerading as Dr. Pascal. Perez then strikes up a conversation with Featherstone as a means to gain the Englishman's confidence. Although no cameras are allowed at the exhibit, Featherstone quietly brags to Perez that he has a hidden camera which he just used to take a picture of the crown.

O'Hara (Harry Strang), a museum guard, is nearby and sees the hidden camera. He struggles with Featherstone to confiscate the camera but it drops to the floor. Recognizing an opportunity to set a trap, Perez deliberately steps on the camera and breaks it, saying it was an accident and is willing to replace it. Perez gives the despondent Featherstone an address of a dealer friend where he would meet him later that evening.

Back at his hotel, Mr. Moto is now getting ready to go out on the town. Unknown to him though, Metaxa is now hiding on a ledge outside his hotel window waiting for a chance to shoot Mr. Moto. Just as he is about to fire his gun, Metaxa is interrupted by the entrance of a hotel bellhop to Moto's room. At the same time, Moto receives an urgent call from Manderson's servant Wong (Honorable Wu), who requests that Moto meet him at the Laughing Buddha, a Chinatown restaurant, because what he has to say can't be said on the telephone. After Metaxa hears Moto mention the caller's name and the restaurant's name where he will meet him, Metaxa quickly leaves the window ledge.

Wong arrives at the restaurant and is seated in a private booth with a closed curtain. A few moments later, Metaxa enters the restaurant and sits in a similar booth next to Wong's. Moto arrives at the restaurant and is led to Wong's booth but he quickly discovers that Wong has been murdered—stabbed in the back by the person sitting in the next booth. The restaurant owner (Victor Wong) and waitress (Iris Wong) quickly assume Mr. Moto is the murderer, and when the waitress screams, Moto quickly exits the restaurant after there is a brief scuffle to capture him.

Now several blocks away from the restaurant, Mr. Moto again unexpectedly runs into Archie Featherstone. "Why, it's Mr. Mot . . . , Mr. Shimako. Funny how we keep bumping into each another," comments the Englishman.

Mr. Moto proclaims the compliment, "Mr. Featherstone, *you are ubiquitous!*" Archie proceeds to tell Mr. Moto about having to go to a shop on Grant Avenue recommended by a Dr. Pascal to get a replacement camera. Both then recognize the address is the same shop where they were previously shot at. Moto deduces that this meeting place is no coincidence but is part of a plan to kill Featherstone as the only person who is able to recognize the gang that stole the armored car. Mr. Moto also realizes that is

Clockwise from the upper left: Lionel Atwill, Victor Varconi, Wille Best, and Joseph Schildkraut.

unsafe to remain there any longer and they quickly get into a cab and head for the Fremont Museum.

Meanwhile in Perez's apartment, Wendling lets Joe Rubla know that, because he is growing suspicious of Perez, he followed him to the museum. Wendling then questions why Perez was at the museum if not planning to steal the crown for himself. Perez returns and is taken by surprise when Rubla asks him how he liked the museum earlier in the day. Thinking quickly, Perez gives the excuse that he was trying to help Rubla by making a sketch of the crown room and the location of the light beams for the alarm system. A gun then carelessly drops from inside Perez's coat to the floor. Believing he is being double-crossed, Rubla fatally stabs Perez with the final reprimand, "You had to learn sometime." Rubla and Wendling then head to the museum to steal the crown themselves.

When Mr. Moto and Featherstone arrive at the museum, Moto identifies himself to O'Hara as being from the International Police and he has urgent business with Prof. Hildebrand. Moto asks O'Hara to call the police, fearing the an attempt will be made to steal the crown that evening, and then heads to the curator's office where Susan French says Hildebrand is in the inner office playing chess with Mr. Manderson.

Inside the office, Mr. Moto informs Manderson that his servant Wong was killed within the hour. When the philanthropist then tries to inform the police, Moto discovers that the telephone wire has been cut—"Someone deprived this instrument of all utility."

Moto then tells the two men about his suspicion that Metaxa will soon attempt to steal the crown. Even though Hildebrand doesn't believe that the famous thief is still alive, Moto assures him Metaxa *is* in San Francisco. Wanting to satisfy himself that the alarm is on if Metaxa is indeed alive, he is horrified to find the alarm controls sabotaged.

Meanwhile at Mr. Moto's request, Featherstone is secretly standing watch in the museum hallway but Paul Borodoff enters the museum and knocks out Featherstone from behind. Now without a working telephone, Hildebrand leads Moto, Manderson, and Miss French to the hallway to find O'Hara and have him summon the police. Instead, they come across Featherstone's unconscious body on the floor. A few moments later, they meet Howard Stevens in the hallway, claiming he had just stopped by to pick up Miss French.

Mr. Moto requests Miss French to stay with Featherstone until he regains consciousness while the rest of them go into Prof. Hildebrand's office to talk. At this time Borodoff, holding a gun, sneaks up behind Susan and tries to force her to tell where the alarm switch is. As Featherstone is regaining consciousness, Susan stalls and tries to signal Archie to hit Borodoff on the head with a bottle. Unfortunately Archie is not quick enough and Borodoff punches him unconscious. Susan bravely grabs at Borodoff's gun and screams for Mr. Moto to help. Moto quickly comes but is fended off by the assailant. Fortunately, Howard Stevens is there to land a punch that knocks out Borodoff.

Prof. Hildebrand recognizes Borodoff and asks Mr. Moto if he could be Metaxa. Moto replies that although Borodoff is a criminal, he is *not* Metaxa. Borodoff and his accomplice Eleanor Kirke are well-known to the English and French police and up to about two months ago, were operating in Shanghai. Finally, Moto reminds Manderson and Hildebrand that besides Metaxa and Borodoff, Joe Rubla also has made an attempt to steal the crown and is still on the lam.

Mr. Moto makes the startling announcement to all that Metaxa is now in the museum—in fact, he is in the room. As a ruse, Moto proceeds to reveal that Manderson's servant Wong had stumbled onto Metaxa's identity and arranged a meeting with him to collect the reward. However Metaxa guessed Wong's intention and stabbed the servant before Moto arrived at the restaurant and could talk with Wong. Mr. Moto further states that Wong was able to inform him of Metaxa's alias before he died. Moto then requests that Prof. Hildebrand accompany him to the police station to be placed under arrest as Metaxa. Outside the museum meanwhile, the police arrive and capture Rubla and Wendling before they are able to get into the museum.

Thinking that the case is now solved, Manderson excuses himself, saying he now wants to get a cab and make arrangements for Wong's funeral. Once out of sight from the others, the viewer now sees Manderson easily run without the aid of a cane towards the vault containing the crown.

With the alarm system disabled, Metaxa having posed as Manderson, grabs the crown and proceeds to make his escape. However, Metaxa is suddenly confronted in the hallway by Mr. Moto holding a gun who warns the master thief that it would be unwise to attempt an escape and he can now stop his characterization of a crotchety old man. Realizing he has been defeated, Metaxa congratulates his victorious adversary on his cleverness. In return, Moto praises Metaxa for his excellent makeup and confesses that his aversion is beards—they itch. Moto further requests the thief now remove his makeup, wig, and glasses so he can see what Metaxa really looks like. Metaxa happily obliges, saying that it will be a relief to be rid of the disguise.

Having now revealed his true appearance, Metaxa requests from Moto the courtesy of how he was able to suspect him. Moto proceeds to point out that the manner by which Wong was murdered was characteristic of Metaxa, but the thief had made one simple blunder. When posing as Manderson, Metaxa arrived at the museum during the rainstorm—the wet footprints in the hallway up to Hildebrand's office were that of a healthy man. Once inside the office however, the footprints changed to that of a man that walked with a noticeable limp. Metaxa again compliments Moto—"You are most ingenious, Mr. Moto. It was stupid of me not to see through your false accusation of Hildebrand."

Suddenly, Metaxa deftly kicks the gun from Moto's hand and, at the conclusion of an exciting fight scene, Metaxa grabs hold of a chandelier, swings through a window to the outside, and falls to the ground below. Before he can get up and escape, Mr. Moto jumps out the window and subdues the thief with handcuffs. Moto requests that Howard Stevens call the police to release Prof. Hildebrand and they are also to pick up Borodoff who is being guarded by O'Hara. As a final caution, Moto tells Stevens to safely secure the ancient crown until the alarm system can be repaired. At the film's end, Moto then reflects on the day's events and ponders aloud, "Oh well. Perhaps I wasn't meant to have a vacation!"

Commentary

By this time, it was apparent that the *Mr. Moto* series was winding down and both the studio and Peter Lorre were going through the motions in the film's production. Mr. Moto now represents the International Police while on the trail of a master jewel thief long thought to be dead. Moto actually has professional respect and admiration for the talents of his foe, many of which are similar to his, for Metaxa is shrewd, displays physical agility, and likes to use disguises.

As with many of the previous entries, *Mr. Moto takes a Vacation* follows the established formula of starting Moto out in one of his disguises, continues with the obligatory development of a romantic interest between a handsome male supporting actor and an attractive female, and the introduction of the comedic foil. In this film, the bumbling misadventures of Archie Featherstone serve to impact the film in a negative manner much the same way as his predecessors did. In hindsight, the weakest films in the series were rife with the unwanted comedy while the best films of the series had none. Museum curator Professor Hildebrand serves as an effective red herring, and his arrest as Metaxa near the film's conclusion serves as a ruse by Mr. Moto to smoke out the real master thief.

B. R. Crisler's review of June 19, 1939 in the *New York Times* sums up the feelings about the *Mr. Moto* series: "In short, the fairest thing one can say for *Mr. Moto takes a Vacation* is that, in this case, it would have been a swell idea." Except for the supporting cast, not much else shows much of any effort. As most fans of the series know, Mr. Moto went on an extended vacation from the silver screen for 26 years until the release of *The Return of Mr. Moto* (1965).

Film Notes

Mr. Moto Takes a Vacation was the eighth and last film of the series with Peter Lorre to be released. However, it was the seventh film in the series to be produced (August 1938), and was released on April 7, 1939, three months after *Mr. Moto in Danger Island*. No reason was ever given by the studio for the seven-month delay.

This film concluded director Norman Foster's association with the *Mr. Moto* series. However, Foster went on to direct three *Charlie Chan* films:

Charlie Chan in Reno (1939), *Charlie Chan at Treasure Island* (1939), and *Charlie Chan in Panama* (1940)—the last two, many fans consider the best of all the *Chan* series. Foster had his wife Sally play the role of Stella Essex along with Cesar Romero (as the murderer) in *Charlie Chan at Treasure Island*.

When in disguise as the Viennese archeologist, Professor Heinrich von Kleinroth, Mr. Moto remarks to an Arabian prince, "Uneasy lies the hand that bears the crown." This is a rephrasing of a line from Shakespeare's *King Henry IV*—"Uneasy lies the head that wears a crown."[44]

Mr. Moto Takes a Vacation has a number of cast members that have worked with Peter Lorre in other films. Hungarian-born Victor Varconi was with Lorre in *Strange Cargo* (1940). Virginia Field, who appears in three *Mr. Moto* films, Lionel Atwill, and Joseph Schildkraut all appeared earlier with Lorre in *Lancer Spy* (1937), which also included future *Mr. Moto* alumni George Sanders and Sig Rumann. Harry Strang was with Lorre in *The Face Behind the Mask* (1941). Although he was never to appear to Lorre again, John "Dusty" King went on to star in many westerns.

---

44   In William Shakespeare's *King Henry IV* (Part II, Act iii, Scene 1), King Henry laments:

> *Canst thou, O partial sleep! give thy repose*
> *To the wet sea-boy in an hour so rude,*
> *And in the calmest and most stillest night,*
> *With all appliances and means to boot,*
> *Deny it to a king? Then, happy low, lie down!*
> *Uneasy lies the head that wears a crown.*

The Return of Mr. Moto (1965)

Lippert Films, Ltd. Distributed by Twentieth Century-Fox Film Corp. Released: October, 1965 (Great Britain); November 3, 1965 (USA). Los Angeles opening: December 29, 1965. Copyright Twentieth Century-Fox Film Corp., 1965; LP32094. Sound: Westrex. B&W. 35 mm. 71 minutes.

Producers: Robert L. Lippert and Jack Parsons. Director: Ernest Morris. Assistant director: Gordon Gillbert. Screenplay: Fred Eggers. Story consultant: Randall Hood. Director of photography: Basil Emmott. Art Director: Harry White. Supervising film editor: Robert Winter. Production manager: Clifton Brandon. Camera operator: Frank Drake. Sound editor: Clive Smith. Sound recordist: Jock May. Music composed by: Douglas Gamley. Hairdresser: Joyce James. Wardrobe supervisor: Jean Fairlie. Make-up: Harold Fletcher. Assistant editor: David Bennett.

Cast

Henry Silva *as*	Mr. Moto [alias Sakura]
Terence Longdon	Jonathan Westering
Suzanne Lloyd	Maxine Powell
Marne Maitland	Wasir Hussein
Stanley Morgan	Inspector [Jim] Halliday
Martin Wyldeck	Dargo [alias for Helmut Engel]
Anthony Booth	Hovath
Brian Coburn	Magda
Peter Zander*	Ginelli
Harold Kasket*	Shahrdar of Wadi Shamar
Gordon Tanner*	Russell McAllister
Henry Gilbert*	David Lennox
Richard Evans*	Chief Inspector Marlow

Dennis Holmes*. . . . . Chapel
Ian Fleming*. . . . . Rogers
Tracy Connell*. . . . . Arab
Alister Williamson* . . . . Maître d'Hôtel
Sonya Benjamin* . . . . Belly dancer

*Uncredited

"No one can run faster than death."

—Dargo to Hovath

The Story

Russell McAllister (Gordon Tanner), an executive of the Beta Oil Company, arrives in London and has dinner with his old friend Mr. Moto. "Mac" tells Moto that one of his company's oil fields in Persia was set afire four months ago as an act of sabotage. It is still burning and losing $100,000 a day, which will virtually prevent Beta from renewing its oil leases with the province of Wadi Shamar. The oilman feels that this is all part of a pattern that will also force other oil companies from the Middle East.

While eating, McAllister appears jumpy and frequently looks over his shoulder. Moto notices McAllister's nervousness and when asked, Mac confides in Moto that he survived an assassination attempt in Persia last week. Interpol promised him that a special agent would contact him in London. To his surprise, Moto tells his friend that he has been talking to *that* agent all evening. Moto then asks why someone would want kill him but the oilman can attribute no specific reason for the attempt. McAllister tells Moto that he feels tired after his trip and will fill him in on the details in the morning.

Waiting outside the restaurant is a stolen cab driven by a gangster named Hovath (Anthony Booth) and in the back seat is a professional hit man named Dargo (Martin Wyldeck). When Moto and McAllister leave the restaurant, Moto says he'll take a stroll while McAllister proceeds to hail a cab. Hovath pulls up to McAllister and Dargo shoots the oilman point blank through the open cab window, killing him instantly. Dargo also shoots at Moto but misses. Nonetheless, Moto falls to the ground as if he were also hit. Dargo knows he missed killing Moto and now needs to quickly find Moto and finish the job. "No one can run faster than death,"

Heny Silva as Mr. Moto in disguise.

Dargo asserts.

While walking around, Mr. Moto notices a slow moving cab following him. He draws the cab to follow him down a dark alley and ducks into a building heading for the roof. Armed with guns fitted with silencers, Dargo orders Hovath to follow Moto inside while he stands guard outside.

Hovath reaches the roof and Moto jumps Hovath. After a brief struggle, Moto captures him at knife point, causing Hovath to confess that he didn't kill McAllister but only drove the cab. Moto also gets him to reveal that he was told which flight McAllister would be arriving on but he doesn't know who hired him—only Dargo knows and he is waiting for Moto downstairs to come out of the building. Hovath suddenly tries to escape, and when he reaches the roof's edge, is shot from below by Dargo. Moto then sneaks down from the roof and escapes in the abandoned cab just before Dargo can catch up with him.

Next morning, Moto sees Ginelli (Peter Zander), another Interpol agent, who tells Moto that Scotland Yard was not able to get any usable fingerprints from either McAllister's hotel room or the cab. Ginelli pledges to arrange for Moto to meet with Scotland Yard's Chief Inspector Marlow to officially provide Interpol with whatever information Moto needs. Moto tells Ginelli that he and McAllister once worked in intelligence together and that Mac had saved Moto's life. Since he can't repay the deed now, Moto vows to get Mac's killer. Moto mentions that all he has to go on is the name *Dargo* and after checking their files, Moto and Ginelli discover Dargo's real identity—Helmut Engel, who is an ex-Nazi SS officer currently wanted by the War Crimes Commission for murder.

Meanwhile, Dargo is meeting with Wasir Hussein (Marne Maitland), who is part of a syndicate attempting to put Beta Oil out of business, take over every major oil lease in the Persian Gulf, and eventually the rest of the world. Also present is Magda (Brian Coburn), a Hussein henchman who calls Dargo an imbecile for failing to kill Moto and remarks that a juvenile fresh out of reform school could have done better. Insulted, Dargo pulls out a gun and lectures Magda with his twisted brand of humor—"In the stomach, one dies very thirsty and slowly, like a plant dried out in the Sahara sun. In the old days I heard the screams, like music of a happy, gay polka. Perhaps with you, I make polka music?" Hussein verbally separates the two and warns they must concentrate on Moto. "We cannot afford this luxury of self-destruction" says Hussein.

Ginelli and Inspector Marlow (Richard Evans) accompany Moto to McAllister's hotel room and check for possible clues. Ginelli sees a memo from the Foreign Office on a table concerning an upcoming oil conference. Marlow explains it is a routine security request, as the Yard covers any meeting involving foreign delegates. Moto is then handed a list of the countries that will be represented—United States, Great Britain, France, Japan. "Not much of a list," Moto remarks, but Marlow replies, "I don't think that most nations look on oil as one of the world's major problems at the moment."[45]

Inspector Marlow then mentions that because McAllister was to represent the United States at the conference, he now will be replaced by David Lennox, the board chairman of Beta Oil. Moto also notices that the Shahrdar of Wadi Shamar will represent the Middle East. As Interpol's representative, Moto tells Marlow he would appreciate his assistance, but Marlow quips, "You mean that ruddy Gunga Din chap?"[46] Moto curtly reminds the chief inspector "that ruddy Gunga Din chap" controls the Beta Oil leases—the only possible motive for McAllister's death. Marlow then says he'll assign Inspector Halliday from the Yard's Special Branch to help out.

When Marlow is about to leave, he takes a verbal jab at Moto, saying

---

45 Oil may have not been one of the world's problems in 1965, but it certainly was eight years later. On October 17, 1973 OPEC (Organization of the Petroleum Exporting Countries) orchestrated an oil embargo against the West, which created a world-wide oil crisis. The embargo officially lasted until March 18, 1974.

46 *Gunga Din* is a poem composed by British writer Rudyard Kipling, England's first Nobel Prize winner for literature (1907), and concerns a native Hindu slave/water boy who desperately wants to be a "first class soldier" for the British army. The following last three line of the poem are perhaps the best known:

> Though I've belted you and flayed you,
> By the livin' Gawd that made you,
> You're a better man than I am, Gunga Din!

he and Ginelli won't find anything *his* men didn't—"We've been at this business quite a while, you know." Searching McAllister's suitcase anyway, Moto notices a carton of cigarettes, and because he knows that his friend McAllister didn't smoke, carefully examines the carton. Inside one of the packs, Moto finds one cigarette that feels like a hollow tube.

Suddenly, Jonathan Westering (Terence Longdon), of British intelligence, arrives and informs Moto and Ginelli that he has been appointed the "unofficial host without portfolio" since the oil conference is being held at his home, Westering Manor. Westering then leaves for the airport to meet Lennox, giving Moto now a chance to examine the bogus cigarette he found earlier. Inside, he finds a rolled-up piece of paper with a list of items written in some sort of code neither Moto nor Ginelli recognize.

When Moto and Ginelli leave McAllister's hotel and they walk down a street, they are followed by a car. As the two enter an intersection, the car

Martin Wyldeck threatens Suzanne Lloyd.

speeds up, narrowly missing hitting Moto. He thanks Ginelli for his quick action saying, "I owe you a spaghetti dinner." Ginelli responds, "I hate spaghetti. Make it a bottle of Scotch!" Having not seen who was driving the car, Ginelli also cautions Moto, "They must want you *real bad*."

Mr. Moto arrives at Westering Manor later that day where he meets David Lennox (Henry Gilbert) and his very attractive secretary, Maxine Powell (Suzanne Lloyd). Moto fills him in on the case so far and when shown the coded list found earlier in McAllister's room, Lennox also does not understand their meaning. However Moto says that his friend was onto something and he feels these numbers are the key. Lennox then realizes that his company uses numbers in their shipping codes to reduce radiogram costs and simplify their inventory. Lennox explains McAllister introduced this number system when he first joined the oil company.

Mr. Moto returns to his hotel room and studies the coded list against Beta Oil's inventory code book Lennox loaned him. Suddenly, the doorbell rings. It is Chapel (Dennis Holmes), a Hussein henchman posing as Inspector Halliday. The impostor takes Moto to the Arabian Nights, a waterfront dive where he tells Moto that an informant wants to meet them. After waiting for a while, Moto is then surrounded by several thugs and realizes that the man sitting across the table is not Halliday. Moto is led to side room and is tied and bound to a chair. At Wasir Hussein's direction, Dargo begins to punch Moto in the ribs, attempting to extract information. Despite the repeated punishment, Moto reveals nothing and Hussein then orders Dargo to kill Moto. Chapel helps Dargo to put Moto into a sack and toss him into the Thames. However Moto has a hidden knife which he uses to cut himself free in the water and then swims to safety.

A few hours later in a hospital, Ginelli and the real Inspector Jim Halliday (Stanley Morgan) arrive to see Moto recovering from his near-fatal ordeal. Halliday says that he was hit on the head and left in an alley. When he regained consciousness, he called Ginelli who then went looking for Moto and found him in an emergency hospital. Ginelli mentions the newspapers were informed of Moto's "death"—"Oriental bobby picked out of Thames identified as I. A. Moto," read the headlines. Moto tells Ginelli that he will be attending the oil conference as the Japanese ambassador's personal representative.

Moto returns to his hotel room with Halliday, but before he enters, he notices that someone is inside. Both enter and surprise Miss Powell with Halliday having punched her. She explains that the building manager let her in. Moto tells Maxine that someone thinks they killed him this evening and asks her to help him on the case by telling the conference delegates that she has important information about the Beta Oil case. Moto also wants Halliday to constantly keep an eye on Maxine as her role could be dangerous waiting for someone to make a move. Halliday then receives a telephone call from a stakeout team informing him that three men left the Arabian Nights—two Arabs and a big man. Moto knows these three but none of these men fit Dargo's description and Dargo could still be inside.

Ginelli visits Moto later and tells him Wasir Hussein is a special representative of the Wadi Shamar government and is also the assistant to the country's ruler, the Shahrdar. Furthermore, Ginelli tells Moto that Hussein is the owner of the Arabian Nights, which is used as a front. With the help the Japanese ambassador, who asks that Moto not do anything that would embarrass the government, Ginelli gives Moto identification papers that will identify him as a man named Sakura, the ambassador's personal representative.

At Westering Manor, the delegates begin to arrive for the conference. Moto, now disguised with glasses and a goatee as Sakura, arrives to meet the other delegates to the oil conference. He is introduced to Maxine who doesn't recognize him through the disguise until he quietly reveals his identity to her. The Shahrdar informs Lennox that he will not be renewing the oil leases with Beta Oil. The ruler is also upset because his kingdom depends on Lennox's company producing oil and there have been no profits for the last six months due to the acts of sabotage.

In the Shahrdar's presence, Jonathan Westering mentions that there are others who would make substantial offers for the oil rights in Wadi Shamar. In particular, he mentions the ruler's own special assistant. The ruler admits that he has had negotiations with Hussein and is inclined to accept Hussein's offer—"It is feasible, it is fair, and he is a countryman with the interest of his people at heart."

Just then, Sakura suggests the ruler reconsider his decision because the woman from Beta Oil has certain information that may affect the countries of all the delegates. Despite Hussein's urging to sign their agreement, the Shahrdar also realizes that his decision could affect others and agrees to hold off his decision until the new information is officially discussed at the conference tomorrow.

Later that evening Mr. Moto, disguised as Sakura, and Westering are playing a quiet game of chess when Halliday comes into the study and informs the two that Miss Powell is gone. Westering thinks that Maxine just went for an evening stroll. Halliday assures Sakura that he has looked everywhere and then worries aloud letting it slip that "A kid like that playing Mata Hari."[47] As Sakura, Moto then tries to calm Halliday down before he exposes Moto's entire plan.

Suddenly, Westering receives a telephone call from Maxine who wants to talk to Sakura. Having been kidnapped by Hussein, Maxine is now forced at gun point to lure Sakura to the Arabian Nights, telling him she has uncovered information on the Beta Oil case and needs to see him right away. Before he leaves, Sakura then requests that Westering and Halliday come to the night club later and bring the Shahrdar and Mr. Lennox with him.

Moto enters the night club and calls out Dargo's name. From a back room where he has Maxine bound and gagged, Dargo answers, "I am here, Mr. Sakura." Moto replies to the ex-Nazi, "Correction. I'm not Mr. Sakura, and you're not Dargo. You're Helmut Engel." Dargo is horrified as he thought Moto was dead—"I killed you, Moto." Moto then stealthily moves around the room, forcing Dargo to fire aimlessly and when Dargo is in the open for a brief moment, Moto throws a knife into Dargo's abdomen.

---

47 Mata Hari was the code name of a Dutch spy for Germany during World War I. Her real name was Margaretha Geertruida Zelle (1876-1917). A dancer in Paris, she joined the German secret service in 1907, and during the war she betrayed important military secrets confided to her by the many high Allied officers who were on intimate terms with her. In 1917 she was arrested, convicted, and executed by the French.

Before he dies, Dargo confesses that he killed McAllister on Hussein's orders. Dargo also reveals that McAllister and Hussein argued over splitting the profits of the new oil leases and the two never trusted each other. Once they would have control of the Beta Oil fields, Hussein thought that McAllister would have him killed, but Hussein struck first. To Moto's disbelief, Dargo then declares that it was McAllister who started the oil conspiracy.

David Lennox, the Shahrdar, Hussein, Ginelli, and Halliday arrive and Maxine is freed. While still disguised as Sakura, Moto proceeds to explain the meaning of the code numbers on the slip of paper found in McAllister's room. Part of the number represents a date while another part is the code number of a particular oil field. For each date, Lennox confirms that McAllister was at the location when it was blown up and Wasir Hussein was also there on the same date, which the Shahrdar confirms. Moto then explains the paper is a coded schedule of the entire sabotage campaign and tells Lennox that both McAllister and Hussein were the leaders. Moto then explains the meaning of the list's final two entries: DL423 and SWS424–April 23 and 24, the dates on which David Lennox and the Shahrdar of Wadi Shamar were to be assassinated.

The ruler then turns to his special assistant, angered that Hussein has misused an important trust placed in him and that he will now suffer the consequences. Despite all these revelations, Moto mentions that there is one additional matter to be revealed—the identity of the one person who knew that Inspector Marlow of Scotland Yard had assigned Halliday to work with him and who used his position of trust to obtain all needed information. Moto then turns on the room lights to reveal Jonathan Westering, now standing in the room, as the mastermind.

After all the conspirators are arrested and taken away, Lennox makes it known that all the countries at the conference have agreed the conspiracy will not be made public. The ruler of Wadi of Shamar then promises Lennox that his country will be only too happy to renew the oil leases with Beta Oil. Moto then pleads with Ginelli to give him a month off as he needs the rest, but the Italian says that he just received orders from Geneva for Moto to head to Cairo by the following Monday. Realizing that he still has several days free, Moto then plans to take Maxine on an extended tour of London.

Commentary

Any hopes of reviving the *Mr. Moto* series after a 26-year hiatus were quickly dashed after the film's release. Reviewers generally panned the film with the feeling that it was a film that should not have been made. Other than the name of the central character, there is very little that ties it to the earlier series with Peter Lorre.

Silva, who is of Hispanic heritage, doesn't even *look* Japanese. But to be fair, the Hungarian Lorre didn't fool too many people either but at least he had some physical characteristics in common with the Mr. Moto of Marquand's novels. The film provides very little action, physical or otherwise, and this Moto wannabe dons a not-too-effective disguise consisting of black glasses, mustache, and a goatee. Silva doesn't even speak with any accent that would make the viewer think Mr. Moto is Japanese until putting on the disguise. Also, his old friend McAllister doesn't even call Moto by his first name—whatever it is.

The resurrected Mr. Moto no longer works for the International Police but rather Interpol which most would guess is the same. In much the same way killers try to kill James Bond with exotic methods but fail, Dargo is also too professionally concerned with *how* to kill Moto, to the point of being an obsession, and he botches the assignment.

The story is weak with very little to recommend about it. There are too many red herrings although it is very obvious that Jonathan Westering is the mastermind. Until Dargo confesses however, it is somewhat of a surprise that Moto's friend McAllister was behind the oil conspiracy as he is killed off very early in the film.

Film Notes

Prior to its release, the working title for *The Return of Mr. Moto* was *Mr. Moto and the Persian Oil Case*. The title was probably lifted from an early script–*Mr. Moto in the Persian Oil Fields*–John P. Marquand supposedly wrote after two of his novels were transformed into movies. In May 1935, Marquand traveled in Persia prior to his second trip to the China for the *Saturday Evening Post* and the idea for his *Persian Oil Fields* script was probably as a result of this trip.

Appendix A

Marquand's Published Writings

Magazine Stories

1921

"The Right That Failed," *Saturday Evening Post*, July 23.

1922

"The Unspeakable Gentleman," *Ladies' Home Journal*, February, March, May.
"Only a Few of Us Left," *Saturday Evening Post*, January 14, 21.
"Eight Million Bubbles," *Saturday Evening Post*, January 28.
"Different from Other Girls," *Ladies' Home Journal*, July.
"How Willie Came Across," *Saturday Evening Post*, July 8.
"The Land of Bunk," *Saturday Evening Post*, September 16.
"Captain of His Soul," *Saturday Evening Post*, November 4.

1923

"The Ship," *Scribner's Magazine*, January.
"The Sunbeam," Saturday *Evening Post*, January 20.
"By the Board," Saturday *Evening Post*, March 17.

1924

"The Jervis Furniture," *Saturday Evening Post*, April 26.
"The Black Cargo," *Saturday Evening Post*, September 20 through October 18.
"Pozzi of Perugia," *Saturday Evening Post*, November 8 through 22.
"A Friend of the Family," *Saturday Evening Post*, December 13.

1925

"The Educated Money," *Saturday Evening Post*, February 14.
"The Big Guys," *Saturday Evening Post*, February 21.
"The Foot of the Class," *Saturday Evening Post*, March 21.
"Much Too Clever," *Saturday Evening Post*, April 25.
"The Old Man," *Saturday Evening Post*, June 6.
"The Jamaica Road," *Saturday Evening Post*, July 4.

"The Last of the Hoopwells," *Saturday Evening Post*, December 5.

1926

"Fun and Neighbors," *Saturday Evening Post*, February 20.
"A Thousand in the Bank," *Saturday Evening Post*, May 1.
"The Tea Leaves," *Saturday Evening Post*, May 8.
"The Blame of Youth," *Saturday Evening Post*, May 29.
"The Spitting Cat," *Saturday Evening Post*, July 3.
"Good Morning, Major," *Saturday Evening Post*, December 11.

1927

"The Artistic Touch," *Saturday Evening Post*, February 19.
"The Cinderella Motif," *Saturday Evening Post*, March 5.
"Once and Always," *Saturday Evening Post*, April 9.
"Lord Chesterfield," *Saturday Evening Post*, June 18.
"The Unknown Hero," *Saturday Evening Post*, July 30.
"The Harvard Square Student," *Saturday Evening Post*, December 10.

1928

"The Last of the Tories," *Saturday Evening Post*, March 24.
"As the Case May Be," *Saturday Evening Post*, June 16.
"Do Tell Me, Doctor Johnson," *Saturday Evening Post*, July 14.
"Three Rousing Cheers," *Cosmopolitan*, August.
"Aye, in the Catalogue," *Saturday Evening Post*, August 11.
"The Good Black Sheep," *Saturday Evening Post*, August 25.

1929

"Warning Hill," *Saturday Evening Post*, March 23 through April 20.
"End of the Story," *Collier's*, April 6.
"Oh, Major, Major," *Saturday Evening Post* April 27.
"Mr. Goof," *Saturday Evening Post*, May 4.
"Rain of Right," *Saturday Evening Post*, May 11.
"And Another Redskin—," *Saturday Evening Post*, May 18.
"Darkest Horse" *Saturday Evening Post*, May 25.
"The Powaw's Head," *Saturday Evening Post*, July 20.

1930

"Bobby Shaftoe," *Saturday Evening Post*, February 8.
"Leave Her, Johnny—Leave Her," *Saturday Evening Post*, March 15.
"Simon Pure," *Collier's*, July 5.
"The Same Things," *Saturday Evening Post* August 2.
"The Master of the House," *Saturday Evening Post*, September 27.
"There is a Destiny," *Saturday Evening Post*, November 8.
"Rainbows," *Saturday Evening Post*, December 20.

1931

"Golden Lads," *Saturday Evening Post*, February 14.
"All Play," *Woman's Home Companion*, April.
"Upstairs," *Saturday Evening Post*, August 8.
"Tolerance," *Saturday Evening Post*, October 17.
"Gentlemen Ride," *Saturday Evening Post*, November 7.
"Call Me Joe," *Saturday Evening Post*, November 28.

1932

"Ask Him," *Saturday Evening Post*, January 23.
"The Music," *Saturday Evening Post*, February 6.
"Deep Water," *Saturday Evening Post*, February 20.
"Sold South," *Saturday Evening Post*, March 12.
"Jine the Cavalry," *Saturday Evening Post*, April 16.
"Jack Still," *Saturday Evening Post*, June 11.
"Far Away," *Saturday Evening Post;* August 13.
"High Tide," *Saturday Evening Post*, October 8.
"Dispatch Box No. 3," *Saturday Evening Post*, November 5.
"Fourth Down," *Saturday Evening Post*, November 19.

1933

"Number One Good Girl," *Saturday Evening Post*, October 14.

1934

"Winner Take All," *Saturday Evening Post*, January 20 through February 17.
"Davy Jones," *Saturday Evening Post*, March 3.
"Blockade," *Saturday Evening Post*, March 24.
"Step Easy, Stranger," *Saturday Evening Post* April 14.
"Lord and Master," *Collier's*, April 21.
"Time for Us to Go," *Saturday Evening Post*, April 28.
"Take the Man Away," *Saturday Evening Post*, May 12.
"Back Pay," *American Magazine*, August.
"Ming Yellow," *Saturday Evening Post*, December 8 through January 12, 1935.

1935

"Mr. Moto Takes a Hand," *Saturday Evening Post*, March 30 through May 4.
"Sea Change," *Saturday Evening Post*, May 25.
"A Flutter in Continentals," *Saturday Evening Post*, June 8.
"You Can't Do That," *Saturday Evening Post*, June 22.
"What's It Get You?" *Saturday Evening Post*, July 13.

"Yankee Notion," *Saturday Evening Post*, November 2.

1936

"Thank You, Mr. Moto," *Saturday Evening Post*, February 8 through March 14.

"Hang It on the Horn," *Saturday Evening Post*, March 21.

"No One Ever Would," *Saturday Evening Post*, April 7.

"A Young Man of Great Promise," *Liberty*, June 13.

"Put Those Things Away," *Saturday Evening Post*, June 20.

"The Road Turns Back: The Author in Search of Earthly Paradise," Forum, September.

"Think Fast, Mr. Moto," *Saturday Evening Post*, September 12 through October 17.

"Don't You Cry for Me," *Saturday Evening Post*, November 21.

"Troy Weight," *Saturday Evening Post*, December 5.

"The Late George Apley," *Saturday Evening Post*, November 28 through January 9, 1937.

1937

"The Marches Always Pay," *Saturday Evening Post*, January 30.

"The Maharajah's Flower," *Saturday Evening Post*, March 27.

"3-3-8," *Saturday Evening Post*, April 10 through May 15.

"Just Break the News," *Saturday Evening Post*, July 3.

"Pull, Pull Together," *Saturday Evening Post*, July 24.

"Everything Is Fine," *Collier's*, October 9.

1938

"Castle Sinister," *Collier's*, February 12 through March 26.

"Shirt Giver," *Saturday Evening Post*, April 30.

"Mr. Moto Is So Sorry," *Saturday Evening Post*, July 2 through August 13.

1939

"Wickford Point," *Saturday Evening Post*, January 28 through March 11.

"Beginning Now–," *Saturday Evening Post*, April 8.

"Do You Know the Brills?" *Saturday Review of Literature*, April 29.

"Don't Ask Questions," *Saturday Evening Post*, September 30 through November 11.

1940

"Gone Tomorrow," *McCall's*, September through January, 1941.

"Come On, Prince," *McCall's*, March.

"March On, He Said," *Saturday Evening Post*, June 29.
"Children's Page," *Saturday Evening Post*, August 31.

1941

"My Boston: A Note on the City by Its Best Critic," *Life*, March 24.
"These Are People Like Ourselves," *Asia*, July.
"Mercator Island," *Collier's*, September 6 through October 25.

1942

"Merry Christmas, All," *Cosmopolitan*, January.
"Doctor's Orders," *Collier's*, May 9.
"Taxi Dance," *Good Housekeeping*, May.
"Good Soldiers Can't Be Introverts," *Harper's Bazaar*, June.
"It's Loaded, Mr. Bauer," *Collier's*, June 13 through August 1.

1943

"The Island," *Good House-beeping*, September.
"I Heard an Old Man Say," *Good Housekeeping*, October.

1944

"The End Game," *Good Housekeeping*, March.

1945

"Iwo Jima Before H-Hour," *Harper's Magazine*, May.
"Lunch at Honolulu," *Harper's Magazine*, August.
"Repent in Haste," *Harper's Magazine*, October, November.

1947

"Why the Navy Needs Aspirin," *Harper's Magazine*, August.
"Close to Home," *Good Housekeeping*, November.
"Banking Is an Art," *Atlantic Monthly*, November through January, 1948.

1948

"Point of No Return," *Ladies' Home Journal*, December through April 1949.

1949

"Return Trip to the Stone Age," *Atlantic Monthly*, April.

1950

"Sun, Sea, and Sand," *Cosmopolitan*, May.
"The Gargle Case," *Flair*, August (reprinted from the *Harvard Lampoon*, 1914).

1951

"Melville Goodwin, U.S.A.," *Ladies' Home Journal*, May through December.

1952

"Inquiry into the Military Mind," *New York Times Magazine*, March 30.
"Two's Company," *McCall's*, November.

1953

"Boston," *Holiday*, November.

1954

"Sincerely, Willis Wayde," *Ladies Home Journal*, November through March, 1955.

1955

"'Happy Knoll' Series," *Sports Illustrated*, June through November.

1956

"'Happy Knoll' Series," *Sports Illustrated*, February, May, July, August.
"Apley, Wickford Point, and Pulham: My Early Struggles," *Atlantic Monthly*, September.
"Rendezvous in Tokyo," *Saturday Evening Post*, November 24 through January 12, 1957.

1958

"Women and Thomas Harrow," *Ladies' Home Journal*, July through November.

Books

The Unspeakable Gentleman, Charles Scribner's Sons, 1922.

Four of a Kind ("The Right That Failed," "Different from Other Girls," "Eight Million Bubbles," "Only a Few of Us Left"), Charles Scribner's Sons, 1923.

The Black Cargo, Charles Scribner's Sons, 1925.

Lord Timothy Dexter of Newburyport, Mass. Minton, Balch & Company, 1925.

Warning Hill, Little, Brown and Company, 1930.

Haven's End, Little, Brown and Company, 1933.

Ming Yellow, Little, Brown and Company, 1935.

No Hero, Little, Brown and Company, 1935.

Thank You, Mr. Moto, Little, Brown and Company, 1937.

The Late George Apley, Little, Brown and Company, 1937.

Think Fast, Mr. Moto, Little, Brown and Company, 1937.

Mr. Moto Is So Sorry, Little, Brown and Company, 1938.

Mr. Moto's Three Aces: A John P. Marquand Omnibus. (*Thank You, Mr. Moto*; *Think Fast, Mr. Moto*; and *Mr. Moto Is So Sorry*), Little, Brown and Company, 1938.

Wickford Point, Little, Brown and Company, 1938.

H. M. Pulham Esquire (from "Gone Tomorrow"), Little, Brown and Company, 1941.

Last Laugh Mr. Moto (from "Mercator Island"), Little, Brown and Company, 1942.

So Little Time, Little, Brown and Company, 1943.

Repent in Haste, Little, Brown and Company, 1945.

B. F.'s Daughter, Little, Brown and Company, 1946.

Point of No Return (incorporating "Banking Is an Art"), Little, Brown and Company, 1949.

Melville Goodwin, U.S.A., Little, Brown and Company, 1951.

Sincerely, Willis Wayde, Little, Brown and Company, 1955.

North of Grand Central: Three Novels of New England (*The Late George Apley*; *Wickford Point*, and *H. M. Pulham, Esquire*), Little, Brown and Company,

1956.

Life at Happy Knoll (collected from *Sports Illustrated*), Little, Brown and Company, 1957.

Stopover: Tokyo (from "Rendezvous in Tokyo"), Little, Brown and Company, 1957.

Women and Thomas Harrow, Little, Brown and Company, 1958.

Timothy Dexter, Revisited, Little, Brown and Company, 1960.

Marquand's Mr. Moto Writings

There is often some confusion when comparing the Mr. Moto titles of Marquand's published serializations, books, and reissued paperbacks. The following is adapted from *John P. Marquand and Mr. Moto: Spy Adventures and Detective Films* by Richard Wires.

Serialization Title	Original Book Title*	Reissued Paperback Title**
No Hero (1935)[a]	No Hero (1935)	Your Turn, Mr. Moto (1985)
Thank You, Mr. Moto (1936)[b]	Thank You, Mr. Moto (1936)	Thank You, Mr. Moto (1985)
Think Fast, Mr. Moto (1936)[c]	Think Fast, Mr. Moto (1937)	Think Fast, Mr. Moto (1986)
Mr. Moto Is So Sorry (1938)[d]	Mr. Moto Is So Sorry (1938)	Mr. Moto Is So Sorry (1986)
Mercador Island (1941)[e]	Last Laugh Mr. Moto (1942)	Last Laugh Mr. Moto (1986)
Rendezvous in Tokyo (1956)[f]	Stopover: Tokyo (1957)	Right You Are, Mr. Moto (1986)

Anthologies

Mr. Moto's Three Aces: A John P. Marquand Omnibus. Boston: Little, Brown and Company, 1938. This volume contains: *Thank You, Mr. Moto*; *Think Fast, Mr. Moto*; and *Mr. Moto Is So Sorry*.

Mr. Moto: Four Complete Novels. New York: Avnel Books, 1983. This volume contains: *Your Turn, Mr. Moto*; *Think Fast, Mr. Moto*; *Mr. Moto Is So Sorry*; and *Right You Are, Mr. Moto*.

Notes:
[*] All titles published by Little, Brown and Company (Boston).
[**] All titles published by Little, Brown and Company (Boston).

a *Saturday Evening Post.* March 30 through May 4, 1935. Six installments.

b *Saturday Evening Post.* Feb. 8 through March 14, 1936. Six installments.

c *Saturday Evening Post.* Sept. 12 through Oct. 17, 1936. Six installments.

d *Saturday Evening Post.* July 2 through Aug.13, 1938. Seven installments.

e *Collier's.* Sept. 6 through Oct. 25, 1941. Eight installments.

f *Saturday Evening Post.* Nov. 24, 1956 through Jan. 12, 1957. Eight installments.

Appendix B

Alternate Titles for Mr. Moto Films

During production, many of the *Mr. Moto* films often had one or more alternate titles. These included: working titles, on-screen titles, and secondary titles used in advertisements or foreign countries.

Release Title	Alternate Title(s)
Think Fast, Mr. Moto	None known
Thank You, Mr. Moto	None known
Mr. Moto's Gamble	*Mr. Moto at the Ringside, Mr. Moto's Diary, Charlie Chan at the Ringside, Charlie Chan at the Arena, Charlie Chan at the Fights*
Mr. Moto Takes a Chance	*Look Out, Mr. Moto*
Mysterious Mr. Moto	*Mysterious Mr. Moto of Devil's Island*
Mr. Moto's Last Warning	*Mr. Moto in Egypt, Mr. Moto No. 6, Winter Garden*
Mr. Moto in Danger Island	*Mr. Moto in Puerto Rico, Mr. Moto in Trinidad, Danger Island, Mr. Moto on Danger Island (UK), Charlie Chan in Trinidad*
Mr. Moto Takes a Vacation	None known
The Return of Mr. Moto	*Mr. Moto and the Persian Oil Case*

Appendix C

Multiple Appearances of Cast Members in Mr. Moto Films

The following is a compilation of those actors and actresses, excluding Peter Lorre, who have been identified as having appeared in two or more of the *Mr. Moto* films. This list was compiled using both the onscreen credits from the films themselves and information from both the *American Film Institute Catalog of Motion Pictures Produced in the United States* and the Call Bureau Cast Service lists for uncredited roles.

3 appearances

Jimmy Aubrey	*Mysterious Mr. Moto; Mr. Moto's Last Warning; Mr. Moto Takes a Vacation*
Lester Dorr	*Mr. Moto's Gamble; Mr. Moto in Danger Island; Mr. Moto Takes a Vacation*
Ralph Dunn	*Mr. Moto's Gamble; Mr. Moto in Danger Island;* Mr. *Moto Takes a Vacation*
Virginia Field	*Think Fast, Mr. Moto; Mr. Moto's Last Warning; Mr. Moto Takes a Vacation*
Leyland Hodgson	*Mysterious Mr. Moto; Mr. Moto's Last Warning; Mr. Moto Takes a Vacation*
Gloria Roy	*Mr. Moto's Gamble; Mr. Moto Takes a Chance; Mr. Moto in Danger Island*
Harry Strang	*Mr. Moto's Gamble; Mr. Moto in Danger Island; Mr. Moto Takes a Vacation*
Frederick Vogeding	*Think Fast, Mr. Moto; Mr. Moto Takes a Chance; Mysterious Mr. Moto*

2 appearances

Leon Ames	*Mysterious Mr. Moto; Mr. Moto in Danger Island*
Thomas Beck	*Think Fast, Mr. Moto; Thank You, Mr. Moto*
Willie Best	*Mr. Moto in Danger Island; Mr. Moto Takes a Vacation*
John Bleifer	*Thank You, Mr. Moto; Mr. Moto Takes a Vacation*
Stanley Blystone	*Mr. Moto's Gamble; Mr. Moto Takes a Vacation*
Ward Bond	*Mr. Moto's Gamble; Mr. Moto in Danger Island*

Charles D. Brown	*Mr. Moto's Gamble; Mr. Moto in Danger Island*
John Carradine	*Thank You, Mr. Moto; Mr. Moto's Last Warning*
George Chandler	*Mr. Moto's Gamble; Mr. Moto Takes a Vacation*
John Davidson	*Mr. Moto's Last Warning; Mr. Moto Takes a Vacation*
Major Sam Harris	*Mysterious Mr. Moto; Mr. Moto Takes a Vacation*
Harold Huber	*Mr. Moto's Gamble; Mysterious Mr. Moto*
Al Kikume	*Mr. Moto Takes a Chance; Mr. Moto in Danger Island*
Isabel La Mal	*Think Fast, Mr. Moto; Mr. Moto Takes a Vacation*
James B. Leong	*Thank You, Mr. Moto; Mr. Moto Takes a Chance*
George Magrill	*Mr. Moto's Gamble; Mr. Moto in Danger Island*
Edward Marr	*Mr. Moto's Gamble; Mr. Moto in Danger Island*
Pat O'Malley	*Mysterious Mr. Moto; Mr. Moto Takes a Vacation*
Lee Phelps	*Think Fast, Mr. Moto; Mr. Moto Takes a Vacation*
Jayne Regan	*Thank You, Mr. Moto; Mr. Moto's Gamble*
Bert Roach	*Think Fast, Mr. Moto; Mr. Moto's Last Warning*
John Rogers	*Think Fast, Mr. Moto; Mysterious Mr. Moto*
Sig Rumann	*Think Fast, Mr. Moto; Thank You, Mr. Moto*
Dick Rush	*Mr. Moto's Gamble; Mysterious Mr. Moto*
Lee Shumway	*Mr. Moto's Gamble; Mr. Moto in Danger Island*
Edwin Stanley	*Mr. Moto's Gamble; Mr. Moto in Danger Island*
Jack Stoney	*Mr. Moto's Gamble; Mr. Moto in Danger Island*
Max Wagner	*Mr. Moto's Gamble; Mr. Moto in Danger Island*

References

Books

Alvarez, Max Joseph. *Index to Motion Pictures Reviewed by Variety, 1907-1980.* Metuchen, N.J: Scarecrow Press, 1982.

Bell, Millicent. *Marquand: An American Life.* Boston: Little, Brown, and Company, 1979.

Birmingham, Stephen. *The Late John Marquand: A Biography.* Philadelphia: J.B. Lippincott Company, 1972.

Coursodon, Jean-Pierre and Pierre Sauvage. *American Directors (Volume 1).* New York: McGraw-Hill Book Company, 1983.

DeAndrea, William L. *Encyclopedia Mysteriosa: A Comprehensive Guide to the Art of Detection in Print, Film, Radio, and Television.* New York: Prentice Hall, 1994.

Dixon, Wheeler W. *The "B" Directors, A Biographical Dictionary.* Metuchen, NJ: Scarecrow Press, Inc., 1985.

Everson, William K. *The Detective in Film.* Secaucus, NJ: The Citadel Press, 1972.

Freese, Gene Scott. *Hollywood Stunt Performers.* Jefferson, NC: McFarland & Co., Inc., 1998.

Gevinson, Alan (Ed.). *The American Film Institute Catalog. Within Our Gates: Ethnicity in*

American Feature Films, 1911-1960. Berkeley: University of California Press, 1997.

Gross, John J. *John P. Marquand.* New York: Twayne Publishers, Inc., 1963.

Hanke, Ken. *Charlie Chan at the Movies: History, Filmography, and Criticism.* Jefferson, NC: McFarland & Co., Inc., 1989.

Hanson, Patricia Kay (Exec. Ed.). *The American Film Institute Catalog of Motion Pictures Produced in the United States. Feature Films, 1931-1940 (Volume F3).* Berkeley: University of California Press, 1993.

Hurst, Walter E. and Richard D. Baer (Ed.). *Film Superlist: Motion Pictures in the U.S. Public Domain, 1940-1949* (Vol. 2). Hollywood: Hollywood Film Archive, 1994.

Katz, Ephraim. *The Film Encyclopedia* (2nd Edition). New York: HarperCollins, 1994.

Krafsur, Richard P. (Ed.). *The American Film Institute Catalog: Feature Films, 1961-70* (Volume F6). New York: R.R. Bowker Company, 1976.

Langman, Larry. *Encyclopedia of American Spy Films*. New York: Garland Publishing, Inc., 1990.

Langman, Larry. *A Guide to the American Crime Films of the Thirties.* Westport, CT: Greenwood Press, 1995.

Marquand, John P. *No Hero*. Boston: Little Brown and Company, 1935.

_____. *Thank You, Mr. Moto*. Boston: Little Brown and Company, 1936, 1985.

_____. *Think Fast, Mr. Moto*. Boston: Little Brown and Company, 1937, 1985.

_____. *Mr. Moto is So Sorry*. Boston: Little Brown and Company, 1938, 1986.

_____. *Last Laugh, Mr. Moto*. Boston: Little Brown and Company, 1942, 1986.

_____. *Stopover: Tokyo*. Boston: Little Brown and Company, 1957.

_____. *Your Turn, Mr. Moto*. Boston: Little Brown and Company, 1985.

_____. *Right You Are, Mr. Moto*. Boston: Little Brown and Company, 1986

The New York Times Film Reviews, 1913-1968 (6 Volumes). New York: The New York Times and Arno Press, 1970.

Palmer, Scott. *British Film Actor's Credits, 1895-1987*. Jefferson, NC: McFarland & Co., Inc., 1988.

Parish, James Robert. *Film Directors: A Guide to Their American Films*. Metuchen, NJ: Scarecrow Press, Inc., 1974.

Parish, James Robert and Michael R. Pitts. *The Great Spy Pictures*. Metuchen, NJ: Scarecrow Press, Inc., 1974.

_____. *The Great Detective Pictures*. Metuchen, NJ: Scarecrow Press, Inc., 1990.

Pitts, Michael R. *Famous Movie Detectives*. Metuchen, NJ: Scarecrow Press, Inc., 1979.

_____. *Famous Movie Detectives II*. Metuchen, NJ: Scarecrow Press, Inc., 1991.

Sherman, Vincent. *Studio Affairs: My Life as a Film Director*. Lexington, KY: The University Press of Kentucky, 1996.

Solomon, Aubrey. *Twentieth Century-Fox: A Corporate and Financial History*. Metuchen, NJ: Scarecrow Press, Inc., 1988.

Steinbrunner, Chris and Otto Penzler (Eds). *Encyclopedia of Mystery and Detection*. New York: McGraw-Hill Book Company, 1976.

Svehla, Gary J. and Susan Svehla (Eds.). *Peter Lorre*. Baltimore, MD: Midnight Marquee Press, Inc., 1999.

Tuska, Jon. *The Detective in Hollywood*. Garden City, NY: Doubleday & Company, 1978.

Tuska, Jon. *In Manors and Alleys: A Casebook on the American Detective Film*. New York: Greenwood Press, 1988.

Vazzana, Eugene Michael. *Silent Film Necrology: Births and Deaths of Over 9000 Performers Directors, Producers, and Other Filmmakers of the Silent Era, Through 1993*. Jefferson, NC: McFarland & Co., Inc., 1995.

Wires, Richard. *John P. Marquand and Mr. Moto: Spy Adventures and Detective Films*. Muncie, Indiana: Ball State University, 1990.

Youngkin, Stephen, D., James Bigwood, and Raymond Cabana Jr. *The Films of Peter Lorre*. Secaucus, NJ: The Citadel Press, 1982.

Zinman, David. *Saturday Afternoon at the Bijou*. New Rochelle, NY: Arlington House, 1973.

Magazines, Newspapers, and Periodicals

Charles P. Mitchell. "A Guide to the Mr. Moto Films." *Classic Images*, April, 1998 (Vol 274), pp. 32, C-1 - C-4.

"Why Did Mr. Moto Disappear?" *Newsweek*. January 21, 1957, p. 106.

Internet Resources/Databases

(Because of the dynamic nature of the Internet/World Wide Web, the following URLs may change or be removed without notice.)

All-Movie Guide. http://allmovie.com

Internet Movie Database (IMDb). http://us.imdb.com

Printed in the United States
59688LVS00005B/142-144